Storytelling
with
Rubber Stamps

by Joanna Campbell Slan
columnist for

Keepsakes
CREATING
SCRAPBOOK MAGAZINE

Books by Joanna Slan:

Scrapbook Storytelling (EFG)

Scrapbook Storytelling: Storytelling with Rubber Stamps (EFG)

Using Stories and Humor: Grab Your Audience (Allyn & Bacon)

I'm Too Blessed to Be Depressed (Wildhorse Creek Press)

Contributions by Joanna Slan

"Directory Assistance"
4th Course of Chicken Soup for the Soul

"Damaged Goods"
Chicken Soup for the Couple's Soul

"Climbing the Stairway to Heaven"
Chicken Soup for the Soul at Work

"The Scar"
Chicken Soup for a Woman's Soul, Vol. II

"And I Almost Didn't Go", "The Last of the Big, Big Spenders"
Chocolate for a Woman's Soul

"United States of Motherhood"
Chocolate for a Woman's Heart

Chicken Soup for the Expectant Mother's Soul

Cover and inside pages:
Photography and design:
　VIP Graphics
　St. Louis, MO
　(314) 535-1117
Hand sketch:
　Bill Perry

Dedicated to my Aunt Shirley, Shirley Helmly
"Now you know why I was carrying those colored pencils."

Acknowledgements. Thanks to the sales team at F&W Publications, especially Laura Smith for believing in the power of creating a series. Thanks also to the incredible team at Creating Keepsakes Scrapbook Magazine for believing in what I have to say about saving stories and giving me a chance to be a columnist. Many accolades to the manufacturers who sent supplies to showcase. And special thanks to my friends who are parents of the "other" children in my life. You honor me by letting me share in the joy of your children.

Scrapbook Storytelling: Storytelling with Rubber Stamps
Copyright © 2001 Joanna Campbell Slan

04　03　02　01　00　　　5　4　3　2　1

Library of Congress Catalog Card Number 00-10368

ISBN: 1-930500-01-7
First Edition. Printed and bound in the United States of America.

Publisher:
EFG, Inc.
savetales@aol.com
www.scrapbookstorytelling.com

Distributed to the trade by:
Betterway Books & North Light Books
Imprints of F&W Publications
1507 Dana Ave., Cincinnati, OH 45207
(800) 289-0963; fax: (513) 531-4082

Contents

Welcome to the World of Stamping!

TOOLBOX

SUPPLIES USED
Throughout the book, whenever available, I've listed the supplies that I used to create the pages.

STORY STARTERS

In the Story Starter boxes, I'll be asking you questions that may spark an idea for a family story that you haven't yet scrap-booked.

Confession time: I love to eavesdrop. You can learn such interesting stuff from other people. Fortunately, I've had the opportunity to listen to conversations all over the country. Since the publication of my book *Scrapbook Storytelling*, I've visited lots of stamping and scrapbooking stores in cities from one coast to another. Sometimes I go to sign books, but sometimes I visit just to see what's up. I always go to listen.

Hearing fellow scrapbookers discuss what they will and will not buy helps me know what people like, don't like, and don't understand.

One hot July afternoon, I was standing in the scrapbooking aisles of Jeffrey Alan's in Normal, Illinois. Two friends were talking to each other about scrapbooking and stamping. "I draw the line at buying stamps," said one. "I'm scared to death that I'll go crazy spending money on them. I don't know if I'd even enjoy stamping. I don't know how to use them. I'm not even sure they're archivally safe. And besides, what happens if I goof up my pages? I think they're like potato chips. I won't be able to buy just one, and how will I know which ones to buy? I'm sticking to stickers. Those I can handle."

But her friend said, "I love stamps! Once you use a sticker, it's gone. Plus you can make stamps in any color you want. Stamps are indestructible. You can find archivally safe ink for them. I even let my kids play with them while I'm cropping. I can color them, cut them out and even make greeting cards with them. I figure the money I've

Here's Where You Find the "Rest of the Story"

In these boxes, I'll share some of the story behind the story. In each case, using a stamping technique helped me create a page that better supported my story.

Your memory album is about you and yours. It is more than a photo album because it shares precious stories of who we are, how we live and what we deem important. To "work," a page must do more than protect your photos. A page works when it tells a story—your story.

saved on greeting cards covers my stamping costs and then some. Yes, I had to learn to use them but it didn't take long. They're fun."

I could relate to BOTH these women. At first, my stamping efforts yielded partial images. More ink was on my hands than on my pages. Was I going to risk messing up a great page with a rubber stamp. No way!

Now, of course, I'm a convert. I love them. You see, stamps are incredibly versatile. If you aren't much of an artist, stamps can give you talents you never knew you had. Best of all, you become familiar with your stamps and you look forward to using them over and over—like spending time with good friends.

Why You Are Going to Love Stamps

See if you can recognize yourself in this scenario: As I open a freshly developed roll of film, I look at the photos and start to imagine the pages I'll make. I get home, look through my paper and discover none of my paper is exactly right.

If the design is right, the color is wrong. If the color is right, the design is too large or small or not quite right. The stickers I have are cute, but too small or too colorful. Although I have a vague idea of what I would like and a lot of money invested in supplies, I somehow seem to have the "wrong" stuff—at least it's the wrong stuff for the photos I'm holding in my hand.

Every page needs to tell a story. Stories work best when they have clear themes running through them. So do pages. So, the pages with the most impact will be those where every element—from photo to journaling to embellishment—supports the story you're trying to tell. Stamping and stenciling techniques open a new world of versatile ways to get exactly the images you want, in the colors and sizes you need.

How to Use This Book

If you start at the front and work your way through, you'll see that the techniques build on each other. Also, the further you get in this book, the more stamps you'll use per page. That said, you should still be able to start anywhere and find the information you need to create a specific look.

Tip!

It's All About the Story

Here's a story that reminds me of memory albums.

A few years ago, we went to my husband's 20th high school reunion. As we approached the park pavilion with the REUNION banner, my husband whispered, "I don't recognize any of these people."

We chatted with people a bit, but it wasn't until David tried to get past the "I'm fine, how have the years been to you?" that he realized he had no shared history with these people.

We were at the wrong reunion— David's reunion was on the other side of the park.

In your scrapbook, if your pages don't work to preserve stories, you might as well be looking at someone else's album. Rubber stamping helps you move past the the experiences that are common to the special stories, talents and personalities that are unique to those you love.

FOUR LEAF

CLOVER

HUNTING

One fine spring day, I taught Michael how to find four-leaf clovers. On the grounds at the Arch, there were scads. As you can see from the photos, it didn't take him long to spot them. 1999

SUPPLIES USED

Paper:
Keeping Memories Alive

Stamp:
Good Luck, ©1992 All Night Media

Ink:
Dauber Duos by Tsukineko
ColorBox Pigment Brush Pad

Fonts:
CK Fill In
CK Print

? STORY STARTERS

What special skills have you taught your children? What special skills did your parents pass on to you?

Using Stamps to Tell Your Tales

To tell the story of our clover hunt, I needed clover embellishment. The colors of most of the St. Patrick's Day papers overwhelmed my story. So, I used a stamp to create paper that enhanced my tale. The versatility and control you have with stamps is just one reason to add them to your scrapbooking techniques. With a stamp, you can control color and image. Your photos take center stage because you have added elements that compliment rather than compete.

TECHNIQUE: *Creating Patterned Paper*

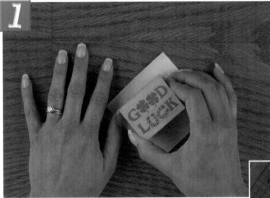

◄ Stamp the image on scrap paper or a Post-it note. Be sure to use a piece of paper large enough to later wrap around the stamp.

Cut out the image you wish to use ► to create your pattern. (You're cutting a window out of the paper to expose what you want to print on your page. The rest of the paper covers the unwanted images.)

◄ Wrap a Post-it Note or your scrap paper around the stamp so that the image you want is exposed. You might wish to tape the paper down and around the stamp. Try only to ink the image you want to print, BUT remember that any ink you get on the paper will dry so quickly it probably won't print on your page.

Sloppy Stamping

Get sloppy. This page is such FUN because it doesn't have to be perfect! In fact, the more imperfect the images, the better.

Use several shades of color to maximize texture on the page, stamping over some of your images.

Put On Shades

When you try several shades, be sure to try black. Black adds great depth to colors. White tones cool color and create pastels. I'm always amazed at how black or gray or white can subtly change colors. When a color doesn't look right, it often begs for an additional helper.

Masking Maximizes Stamp Use

How can you get the most for your money when you buy rubber stamps? After all, rubber stamps can be expensive. So, plan to get as much use as possible from every stamp you buy. Look at your stamps as collages of multiple images, not as one image. Then, experiment with printing singular images or partial images from one stamp.

For me, this masking technique works well. I try to only ink the part of the image I want, but the paper helps when I "color outside of the lines." Because the paper absorbs the extra ink quickly, it minimizes any printing of "unwanted" images. And the paper helps me figure out where to put the ink, since deciphering an image from a stamp face (the die) can be tricky.

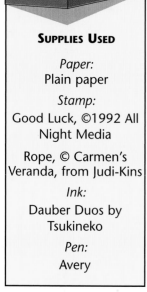

TOOLBOX

SUPPLIES USED

Paper:
Plain paper

Stamp:
Good Luck, ©1992 All Night Media

Rope, © Carmen's Veranda, from Judi-Kins

Ink:
Dauber Duos by Tsukineko

Pen:
Avery

? STORY STARTERS

What hobbies did you enjoy before your children were born that you don't have time for now? It's so good that our children realize we were people before we were parents.

Riding Lessons at FOXTON FARMS. When I lived in Indiana, I took English riding lessons from Jerry at Foxton Farms in West Lafayette. This is probably 1978 or 1979.

Donnegal, My Beautiful Dappled Friend

All the horse-ish paper I found featured brown tones. The patterns I saw overwhelmed Donnegal's soft colors. Again, the "Good Luck" stamp was pressed into service. My photos really stood out against the multi-colored horseshoes on a gray-blue background. By keeping the soft palette of colors, I underscored Donnegal's personality. For all his size and energy, he was a gentle, wonderful horse. *Remember*: Memory is more than photos; it's feelings, too.

TECHNIQUE: *Adding a Journaling Box*

◄ Stamp your image on waste paper or a Post-it note. Cut a window out of the waste paper to expose what you want to print. Wrap the paper around the stamp, exposing the desired image. Ink the desired image and print the image. Repeat in a variety of colors.

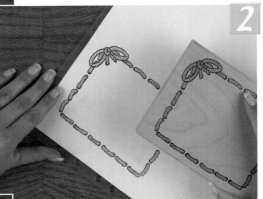

Ink and stamp the frame image on ► a piece of archival paper. Color in your image. Journal inside the box, then cut the box out of the paper.

◄ If desired, add handwritten words to your background stamping. (I added the words "horseshoes" on the page.) Now, adhere the journaling box.

Multiple Uses

Yes, this background was created with the same stamp I used on the Clover page (see page 6). By breaking a stamp down to its basic elements, you maximize your usage potential.

Frame Game

This Rope frame stamp is a fairly neutral stamp. Turn to page 70 and see how different it looks in different colors.

Stamps definitely have a mood. They can be cute, jazzy, sporty, elegant, baby-ish, classic or neutral. The more neutral, the more useful. What makes a stamp neutral? That's a toughie. The best definition I can offer is that a neutral stamp goes with almost everything.

Frame Stamps

Frame stamps are one of the easiest stamp designs to use. They are perfect for matting photos, but they also work well as journaling boxes.

As a rule, you'll want a journaling area equal to the size of one photo for each scrapbook page. Many frame stamps are sized to fit around a standard photo. By planning to set aside this space, even if you journal later, you'll train yourself to include more of your favorite family stories.

SUPPLIES USED

Stamp:
Paw, ©1996
Stampendous!

Ink:
Memory Acid Free
Ink Pad by
Inkadinkado

Marker:
Zig

Do you have a pet who gets into mischief? What does that pet do? Have you caught him or her in the act?

Busted! Doggone it!

Okay, I've got an attitude. I think
my little green tootsies are cool.
Not my fault the boys
forgot I was
outside.

Not my fault mama
was sleeping late.
Not my fault I had
to run through the
freshly mowed grass.
Not my fault it turned
my little legs green.

...ark to get back in the house. Big deal.
...lawn mowers are scary. I did get to
...e." How was I to know I was headed
...y beauty parlor? I have a bone to pick
...e because life just isn't fair!

...th a groomer, Spring, 1999

The Green's the Thing

When I looked for paper for this page, I found dog paw prints. But, gee, none of them were GREEN. Kevin's little green knee socks so tickled me that I couldn't change my mind about the importance of green on this paper. Again, stamping came to the rescue. The paw prints on the border add humor and spark your curiosity. The border helps make the photos stand out more. No need for green paws? Of course, you could do this same design with any stamp design and border template.

TECHNIQUE: *Adding a Stamp to Patterned Paper*

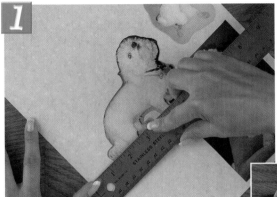

◄ Plan your layout. Crop your photos and place them as desired on the page, but don't adhere them yet. Get the feel of the space for your border. Now use a ruler to see how much border space you have on the left and right sides. Make a pencil mark, or use a Post-it Note to designate the space.

Align the border template with your chosen border. Line up the template parallel with the paper's edge. Trace along the edge of the border template with your marker. Lift the border template straight up so you don't smear your ink. ▶

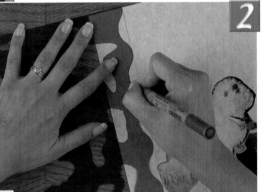

◄ Ink your stamp and stamp your image in between the border template and the outside edge of your paper. You may wish to tilt the image, as I did. Add small "hash" marks to your border line with your pen.

Indexes

That printed image on the back of your stamp handle is called the index. The index has many uses:

1. It helps you quickly identify your stamp since the rubber dies can be hard to decipher.

2. The index helps guide you as you use the stamp, reminding you where the top and bottom are.

3. If the index is colored, it can be used as a model for your coloring efforts.

Trash or Waste Paper

Even with an index, you can get "turned around" as you put down an image. That's why it's so useful to keep a piece of trash paper nearby as you work on your pages. Concerned about how your ink color will look? Wondering which end is top or bottom? Simply stamp your waste paper.

Stamping on Patterned Paper

At first, you may want to stamp on white or cream paper. Then, you may move into pastels. So far, so good. Now take a walk on the wild side and print a stamp on patterned paper. Here are a few guidelines:

1. Use patterned paper that is pastel in colors and stamp on it with a deeper value of the same color or a contrasting color.

2. Use a stamp with a solid image that's bigger than the images of the pattern. A smaller solid image may get lost.

3. If you don't use a solid image, use an image with a bold, simple design so the design will stand out from the pattern.

4. To check and see how your stamp will show up, stamp a portion of the paper that will be under your photo. If you don't like the results, that area will be covered later by a picture.

TOOLBOX

SUPPLIES USED

Paper:
Keeping Memories
Alive

Stamp:
Ruler & Pencil,
© House Mouse
Design,
Stampa Rosa

Ink:
Archival Inks™ by
Ranger Industries

Lettering:
Alphabet Template,
Classic Lower by
Frances Meyer

? STORY STARTERS

*Capture a growth spurt
or document a physical
change. How could you
tell a change was
happening?*

The Summer of 1999 Michael grew at an almost alarming rate. It seemed like every time we turned around, he was taller, but in shorts the change was not easy to track because his pants never seemed much shorter. So David got the idea of making marks on the garage wall and dating them to measure Michael's progress.

6-14	55"
7-27	56"
8-10	57"
11-30	58"

WANTED: Bad Photo Needs Great Illustration

Yeah, this photo of Michael didn't turn out well. The light in the garage was too dim. A stamp is a perfect way to rescue a bad picture, because the stamp becomes the dominant illustration while setting the stage for the story.

Try stamping your images on waste paper and cutting them apart. You might be surprised at the ways your stamps and your photos can interact.

TECHNIQUE: *Customizing a Stamped Image*

◀ Ink all of your image except the numbers on the ruler. (You can use a marker to ink around them or stick a tiny bit of Post-it Note on the numbers.) Stamp the image two times on plain white paper. Let the stamped images dry.

Color in the images with pencils. You'll need to color one entire image (mice and ruler) and only the ruler on a second image. ▶

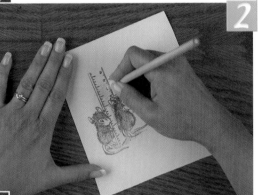

◀ Cut out one entire image. Cut the "mouse with pencil" free from the image. Cut out the ruler from the second image. Add the second ruler to the first ruler to create a longer ruler. Adhere the two ruler pieces together. Add consecutive numbers to your new, long ruler with a fine point marker.

Silhouette crop the photo. Position ▶ the photo on the page with the mice using a movable adhesive such as HERMAfix. Add stairs of solid paper so the mouse on the right isn't floating in space. Add the "mouse with ruler" to the left of your photo.

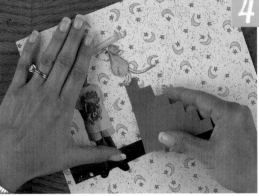

Mistake-Proof Stamping

Scrapbookers often hesitate to start stamping because they are afraid of ruining a page. By stamping on a plain piece of paper, then coloring and cutting your image, you maintain complete control—and your page stays safe.

Stamps as Design Helpers, Not Finished Art

As we photographed this book, Matt, our photographer, said, "I get it. You're using the stamps as guidelines, not as finished art." Wow! He's right. I think of stamps as design helpers. I color over stamps, leave parts out, cut them up and use my marker to change parts of the design. Stamps are tools, not sacred objects.

TOOLBOX

SUPPLIES USED

Paper:
The Paper Patch

Diamond Dust Paper
by Paper Adventures

Stamp:
Millennium Frame,
© All Night Media

Ink:
Paintbox by ColorBox

Embossing Powder:
Hampton Art Stamps

? STORY STARTERS

How and where do you spend your holidays? Do you have a tradition of traveling to a certain spot for certain special days?

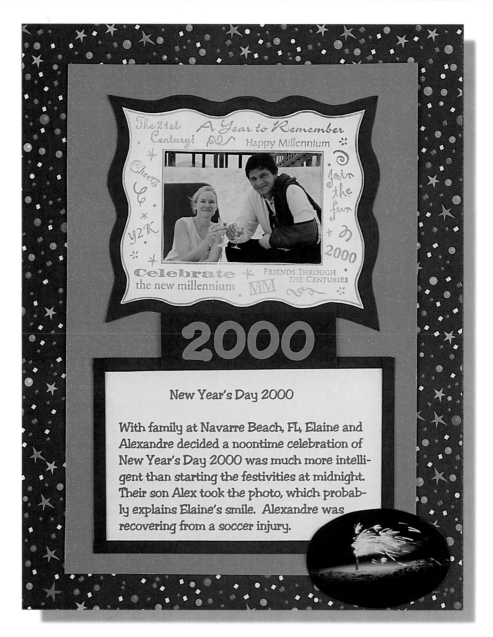

New Year's Day 2000

With family at Navarre Beach, FL, Elaine and Alexandre decided a noontime celebration of New Year's Day 2000 was much more intelligent than starting the festivities at midnight. Their son Alex took the photo, which probably explains Elaine's smile. Alexandre was recovering from a soccer injury.

DESIGN CHALLENGE: Balancing Pastels with Black

*T*he photo of the sparkler was too cool to ignore, but Elaine and Alex were wearing pastels. Hmmm. How to balance extreme dark and light on one page? Stamping the frame in pastels, then backing it with black paper worked. The colors go from pastels in the center to medium hues (the blue) in the middle and end with a black frame sprinkled with color.

What makes it work? The black mat behind the frame and the journaling box.

TECHNIQUES: *Embossing & Framing*

◄ Stamp your framing stamp on waste paper. Cut out the center section with a craft knife. Set the frame over your photo to determine the fit.

Ink your stamp. I used a rainbow stamp pad, but you can use any color. Be sure to choose ink that is pigment not dye. Pigment ink dries slowly so your embossing powder can adhere to it. Stamp your frame on plain white archival paper. ▶

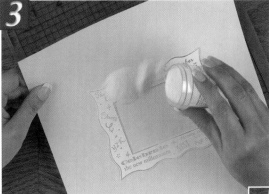

◄ Put a piece of waste paper slightly creased in the middle under your stamped image. Sprinkle clear embossing powder on the image. Tap the side of your stamped paper against the waste paper to shake off unneeded powder. Return unused powder to the container. The crease guides the powder into the container.

Heat the embossing powder. Use an embossing heat gun, or hold your paper over a light bulb or over a toaster. Be careful! Even with the embossing heat gun, you can scorch your paper. Cut out the center of your stamped frame. Adhere it over the photo and to the page. ▶

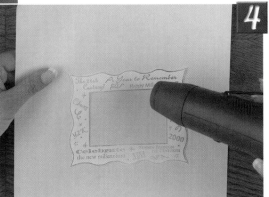

Embossing Tips

1. Pigment inks are best for embossing because the ink dries slowly.

2. If you use a dye ink, experiment with a clear embossing ink over your dye image to hold the embossing powder.

3. Generally, the color of the final image is the color of the embossing powder, *except* if the powder does not completely cover the ink, the ink will show through. Also, white or light embossing powders may let the underneath color show through. This is an important feature because if you don't like your inked image's color, emboss it.

TOOLBOX

SUPPLIES USED

Paper:
Plain gray

Stamp:
Sheep, © 1996 Center Enterprises

Die Cut:
Ellison

Border Template:
Memories Forever

Liquid Applique:
Marvy
Uchida of America

Decorative Scissors:
Paper Adventures

Fonts:
CK Frosting & CK Print

STORY STARTERS

Document your child's sleep patterns. What did your little one wear? What "lovey" did he or she take to bed?

Counting Sheep!

Here is a complete pictorial history of all the times Michael slept before the age of five years. Notice the butt-up-in-the-air pose. Very common. The stuffed toy was to help him get used to Kevin, but Kevin had amorous ideas so we ditched it.

Organizing a Page by Theme to Tell the Story

My son appears in three different ages in these photos, but the theme is always bedtime. You can organize a page in many ways, for example: chronologically, by the subject of the photos, by events, or by theme.

Once you decide on a theme, brainstorm what you associate with that theme. I had these cool sheep die cuts, so I bought the sheep stamp. The color came from Mike's clothes.

TECHNIQUES: *Using Punches & Liquid Applique*

◀ Crop and arrange your collage on the bottom of your paper. Leave about $1/3$ of your page at the top for journaling. Now, measure how much room you have for a border. Use a border template and marker to draw a border. Now stamp your image along the edge of the paper.

Add liquid applique to the bodies ▶ of the sheep. If desired, outline your stamped image with a black archival pen. Let the liquid applique dry. Use the white end of the Dauber Duo to create clouds between sheep by lightly touching the sponge to the paper.

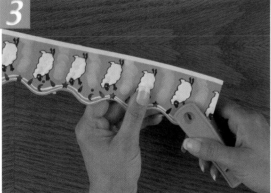

◀ Trim off the excess outside of the border. Mark where you want to punch your design. Line up the punch with your marks. Punch. Add stripes with white archival ink. Slip a piece of white paper beneath the punched border and trim it. Add the border to the page. Use a piece of typewriter correction tape or white paper to create a white border.

Backstamping

Backstamping is the technical name for that little extra image you get when the edge of your stamp die prints on the paper. Here are a few ways to avoid backstamping:

1. Use a craft knife and trim the excess rubber off your stamp die before stamping.

2. Remember to *kiss* your paper with your stamp. Backstamping is more likely to occur when you put a lot of weight behind the stamp and you rock the stamp.

3. Practice with your stamp on waste paper. You'll learn the peculiarities of a particular stamp. They all have them!

Mistakes Happen. Here's What to Do...

Here are my favorite ways to correct mistakes:

1. Sand off the mistake with a nail shaping block. This works really well on white paper.

2. Cover the mistake. The clouds under the sheep happened because I had to cover up a backstamping error.

3. Cut out the stamped image and use it as a sticker. This is a sure cure for backstamping and other nasties.

4. Use typewriting correction fluid. (I'm not sure if it's archivally safe.)

5. Use an archivally safe marker of the same color as your paper.

Line Up!

Turn your punch upside down so you can see your marks through the window of the punch design.

SUPPLIES USED

Paper:
Plain white

Stamp:
Spring Bouquet,
© David

Stencil:
One Heart, One
Mind's Fresh & Funky

Ink:
Inkadinkado

Pens:
Marvy Le Plume II
Zig

Lettering:
Alphabet Template,
Classic Caps by
Frances Meyer

Adhesive:
HERMAfix

Paint:
Delta Paint

Capture a funny family happening. What happened to whom and why? Include photos of the folks involved.

Wear the Rubber Off That Stamp!

Rachel is such a "girly girl." I wanted pink and flowers, but I wanted control of where the images went. Plus, I had a part of this story that is not available for public viewing. (Rachel's mother, my sister, threatened me with—gulp—my life, if I shared it.) So I created a folded "card" to be the journaling box. The background was created by using a Fresh 'n Funky stencil and Delta paints. Then, I used and reused a lovely floral bouquet stamp. I used it as the background for the "R", the embellishment for the journaling card, and the border for the same card.

TECHNIQUE: *Using a Mask with Stamps*

Using a letter template, copy a letter onto waste paper or a Post-it Note to create a mask. A capital letter or a bold lower case letter will give you the best results. Cut out the letter and attach it to a sheet of archival white paper.

Using inks that are water soluble, stamp over the letter and all around it in different colors. I used Marvy LePlume II markers to individually color the flowers and stems on the stamp.

Dip a small brush into water and blot it so that a slight dampness remains on the bristles. Start at the outside edge of the stamped image and draw the ink toward the inside. Continue to paint, using water to reactivate your ink. When dry, remove the mask. Retrace the letter using the letter template and color it in.

Create a decorative border for the bottom of your concealed journaling box which opens like a note card. Put down a piece of waste paper or a Post-it Note the length of your card. Stamp your images along the edge of the waste paper, slightly overlapping each other.

When your border is dry, lift off the waste paper mask. You will have both a straight edge and a jagged floral edge. Use decorative scissors to trim the jagged edge. Trim the straight edge with regular scissors. Add the border to the folded card.

Ink and Think

If you are new to stamping, but not new to crafts or scrapbooking, you probably have many inks you can use on your pages. Here's a rundown of inks and their properties:

Archival—To be truly archival, the ink must be pH neutral, water resistant and fadeproof.

Pigment—A slow drying ink.

Dye—Think "dye and dry." This is a fast drying ink.

Water Soluble— Obviously, if the ink is soluble in water, it is not totally safe for your pages. The solution? Color copy or scan any image made with "non-safe" ink. Of course, then you have to make sure your printer or copier has archival ink.

Embossing Ink—A slow drying ink that holds embossing powder well.

How can you keep all this straight? Just keep reading the information on the product label.

TOOLBOX

SUPPLIES USED

Paper:
Plain yellow

Ink:
White Ink by
ColorBox

ColorBox Pigment
Brush Pad

Pencil:
Berol PrismaColor

Embossing Powder:
Hampton Art Stamps

? STORY STARTERS

Share a child's response to a new food. (Or a young adult's response! I remember my first taste of lobster at age 18.)

Dylan MacFarquhar had never tasted a lemon before! What a surprise. ★ West Palm Beach ★ Spring Break 1998

Makes My Mouth Water. How About Yours?

*O*nce again, I had a great page idea and photo but no paper. So, I found this super-cheap stamp, and I was set. Of course, yellow doesn't show up well. But if you've ever left your lemons out long enough, you know they can turn all sorts of colors. The simple embellishment of the larger slice made for perfect additions. To create the headline, I first traced the letters lightly in the orange color with pencil to make sure I had the overlap just right. Because I did my tracing in orange, I didn't need to erase the tracing when I went over it with a marker.

TECHNIQUE: *Using Multiple Sizes of One Stamp*

◄ Start with the lightest ink color. Ink the stamp and stamp the image on the page. Clean the stamp. Ink the stamp in another color. Repeat with as many colors as desired. Let dry. Now stamp with the color you want to emboss. Sprinkle embossing powder over the page. Tap off the excess. Heat to make the powder rise.

Stamp the image on white paper with black ink. Enlarge the image using one of the methods in the box below. Color in the larger image. ►

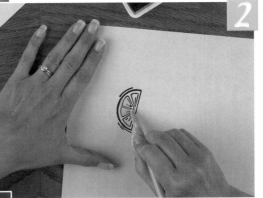

◄ Cut out the larger image after you color it. (*Remember:* Larger pieces of paper are easier to work with than smaller ones. Always try to do your coloring on bigger pieces.) Cut out the larger version of the stamp and adhere it to the page.

Taking Issue with Enlarging

If at all possible, you do NOT want to have to enlarge your stamp yourself. Instead, try to purchase the larger size. Ask your stamp retailer if a larger stamp is available.

Is It a Lemon or a Lime or a Grapefruit?

Beats me. That's what's cool about stamps. I found this fruit slice stamp in a five-and-dime store. There is no descriptive label on it. So, if it's green, it's a lime. If it's orange, it's an orange. If it's yellow, it's a lemon. And if it's pink, guess what? It's a grapefruit. I hope you are much, much smarter than I am, because I was wondering what fruit I had for hours!

Super Size It! Here's How...

1. Photocopy your image at a larger size onto archival paper.*

2. Scan the image and print it out in a larger size.

3. Draw a grid like a tic-tac-toe box over the small image. Draw the same grid larger. Copy the image onto the larger grid one box at a time using images in the small grid as an example.

* Sometimes photocopy powder flakes off as you color it. You may need to re-outline your image. Also, please observe copyright laws.

SUPPLIES USED

Stamp:
Leaves, © Inkadinkado

Ink:
Archival Inks™ by
Ranger Industries

Pencils:
Derwent Watercolour

Embossing Powder:
Hampton Art Stamps

Dots:
Pop it-Up™ Dots by
Cut-It-Up

Do the seasons change
where you live? Ob-
serve the telltale signs.
What's the first part of
nature to signal the
change?

The Subtlety of Early Autumn's Blush

Sure, there are lots of papers and stickers with bright fall colors on them. I didn't want bright fall colors. I had gone to a lot of trouble to photograph the gentle shading that announced fall was coming, and bright colors would have overpowered my photos. With stamps and water-color pencils, I could control the intensity of color, and I did.

Notice there isn't much in the way of journaling here. I simply wanted to capture the beauty of a place my family enjoys.

TECHNIQUE: *Coloring with Watercolor Pencils*

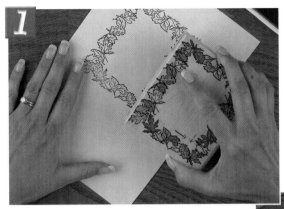

◀ Stamp your frame stamp with archival ink. You may wish to stamp several frame images so you have plenty of the perimeter to use.

Color in the leaves with watercolor ▶ pencils. Use more than one color per leaf for realistic results. It's best to color lightly. Once dry, you can re-color leaves with regular colored pencils or add more watercolor pencil. Use a slightly damp paint-brush to activate the color and smooth the textures.

◀ Cut apart the leaves. (Pieces of two or three leaves work best.) Cut areas between the Pop it-Up Dots in sizes to fit on the back of the leaves. Add Pop it-Up Dot pieces to the backs of the leaves. Press the leaves on the mats around the photos to frame them.

Coloring with Pencils

Even if you aren't artistic, you can get splendid results with colored pencils. Start by coloring with the lightest shades. Add deeper shades over the light ones. In nature, everything is a blend of colors so always use several colors if you want your image to look natural. Be sure to invest in good quality colored pencils. They lay down color more evenly.

"Marrying color" is a term used by makers of hooked rugs. You "marry" colors when you borrow a bit of color from one area and add it to another area. If you are coloring in a leaf on an apple, you might add a little green in the red of the apple—and a little red into the green of the leaves. Done subtly, this makes the entire color scheme more pleasing to the eye.

Pop it-Up Dots

The best tools and ideas are always the simplest. These little gizmos add so much visual punch to your page that you'll love them.

Pop it-Up Dots work well under any embellishments, such as stamped art (as shown), die cuts, lettering, and paper dolls. You can even put them under stickers. To counter-act the sticky backs of the stickers, simply put on the Pop it-Up dots, then dip your finger into a little baby powder and apply the baby powder to the exposed sticky area.

TOOLBOX

SUPPLIES USED

Paper:
Plain cream paper

Stamp:
Heiroglyphics, © 1999
Toybox Rubber Stamps

Chalks:
Decorating Chalks by
Craft-T Products

Pencils:
Derwent Watercolour

Embossing Powder:
Hampton Art Stamps

Doll:
Jill's Paper Dolls

Markers:
Marvy and Zig

? STORY STARTERS

Document a travel
tribulation. What was
unexpected? What was
your reaction?

Sleep Like an Egyptian

Five Star Speakers and Trainers had a showcase in Philadelphia that I attended. When I got to the hotel, the only non-smoking room they had was a "theme" room. The room, Tut's Tomb, was painted like the inside of a pyramid--but tacky! I invited my speaker friends up to see the wild accommodations. We had a great laugh, but it was kind of creepy sleeping in a tomb.

SPRING '99

Below, left: Cindy Kubica
Below, right: me

Sleeping in Tut's Tomb? Weird, Weird, Weird

Of course, there are not a lot of Egyptian scrapbook papers on the market. I used chalk to draw the pyramid blocks on my background paper. The edge of a foam paint brush made the sharp line. I wanted to duplicate the feel of my weird hotel room.

I used a template to cut a paper doll out of a reddish paper and crimped the paper of her dress in a paper crimper. The template for the doll's clothes and hair are with the corner template at www.scrapbookstorytelling.com.

TECHNIQUE: *Using Chalk with Stamps*

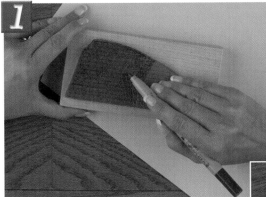

◀ Using a marker, ink the die of the stamp. "Chuff" on the stamp, blowing moist air from the back of your throat to reactivate the ink. Stamp the image and let it dry, if necessary. Repeat until you have four images.

Apply chalk to a sponge applicator or to a cotton swab. Scrub the chalk over the inked image. Use light shades in the beginning, as you can always add more color. ▶

Chalk It Up
My sister Margaret hates chalks but I love them. You'll have to try them for yourself to make up your mind.

Three ways to apply chalk include cotton swabs, sponge applicators like the ones that come in eyeshadow, and brushes.

Because chalks are soft, you can use them over an image and not lose the image. For this project, I used black and tans to get a weathered look.

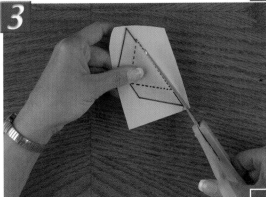

◀ Copy a corner template from the templates at scrapbookstory-telling.com. Or, photocopy and enlarge this page as a pattern. Trace the template onto the back of the stamped image. Go back over the long corner edge with deckle scissors.

Score the fold by running the back of your scissors' blade along it. Fold the flaps toward the inside. Wrap the stamped photo corner around the back of the mat and adjust the fit, if necessary. ▶

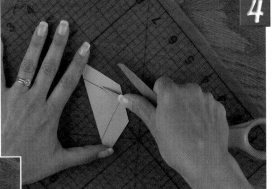

Photo Corners
You can use the photo corner template from scrapbook-storytelling.com to make a photo corner out of almost any-thing: a stamped image, a sticker, a piece of patterned paper or a piece of vellum.

◀ Adhere a photo split to the corner of the stamped image on the backside of your mat. Do this with all four corners. Flip over the mat, and center the photo inside it. Adhere the photo to the mat.

SUPPLIES USED

Paper:
Creative Memories

Stamp:
Stamp: Sun,
© Imaginations

Play and Learn Stamp
Letter Set by Crafts-
Mate

Ink:
Stampin Up!

Pens:
Marvy

Font:

STORY STARTERS

Record a favorite play-
time activity. Did you
need to purchase any
equipment? What did
your child (or even
your pet) do over and
over?

Brighten Up a Dark Day and a Gloomy Photo

I don't know why these photos came out so dark. By cutting out the
background on two photos—or "silhouette cropping" as it's called—and
matting the pictures in bright yellow, I managed to brighten up the
page.

When choosing paper and embellishments, let the colors that dominate
your photo guide your color selections. The yellow and blue in Michael's
clothes and sandbox are repeated in the papers and the headline.

TECHNIQUE: *Using Stamps as Embellishments*

◄ Stamp the sun image in orange on yellow paper to make three copies. Add embossing powder and heat. Cut out the images. Mat on deeper yellow paper. Trim the mat around the suns.

Stamp the letters of the headline. Color in the letters. Correct any problems with the letter outline by using an orange marker. Add dots of orange and slight streaks of yellow. Add one matted sun to the headline. ►

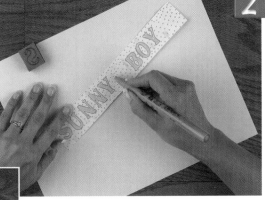

◄ Print your journaling copy using a boldface type style at least 16 points in size. Stamp yellow suns on top of the journaling copy. Trim the journaling boxes.

Outlines and Solids, the Two Families of Stamps

In general, stamps come in two types of images: outlines and solids.

Outlines offer the boundaries of an image. If you want a solid colored shape, you either need to color in the image or stamp the image on colored paper. Because the outline is light, you can stamp over journaling and still see the words.

Solid stamps offer a full surface to ink so that the resulting image is colored in when stamped. One problem with solid stamps is that they can dry out before you get them completely inked. If that happens, simply color in the stamped image with a marker or pencil. You can create a light version of the solid stamp by "off-stamping." To off-stamp, ink your stamp, stamp "off" the extra ink on waste paper and then stamp the lighter image on your final surface.

Tip!

Cheap, Cheap, Cheap

When I began writing this book, I was told that St. Louis (my home) had no stamp stores. A year later I discovered that two art supply stores carried a selection of rubber stamps. Then, a real rubber stamp store opened. (If you are thinking, "A year to write a book?" The answer is, "No, two years.")

In between my discoveries, I searched every nook and cranny for stamps. The "rubber" stamps that make up the letters of this headline were in the $1 bin at my local Toys R Us. For a buck, you can't go too far wrong.

Good quality rubber stamps produce crisp images. However, even cheap stamps can be useful if you are willing to work around their imperfections. With these letters, I often have to go over the outline again in pen.

TOOLBOX

SUPPLIES USED

Paper:
Keeping Memories Alive

Stamp:
Corner Stamp from kit by Rubber Stampede

Journaling Stamp by Scrapbookin' Stamps

Ink:
Archival Inks™ by Ranger Industries

Chalk:
Decorating Chalks by Craft-T Products

Lettering:
Pen Script Lettering Template by Fiskars

Punch:
Crown punch by McGill

? STORY STARTERS

Share the history of a group you were in-volved in. How did you come together? What was your goal? Who was involved?

Womanwriter

In the spring of 1985, a group of want-to-be writers met in an adult class offered by Illinois State University in Normal, IL. Eight of us continued to meet and work on our writing on a regular basis. Although we had our ups and downs, the group gave us all support and a sounding board for our work. We even published a chapbook called A New Line.

Since then I've maintained my friend-ship with Terri Kaminski (Clark). From L-R (first row, above): Jana Suchy, Terri, me, Melanie Verbout. Second row: Carol Etter, Nettie Strohkirch, Terri Ryburn-LaMonte, Marita Brake.

Women with an Attitude

We had a message. All of us wanted to become published writers. First we took a class, and then we met regularly to work on our skills. I wanted this page to focus on our bond, our womanhood. The colors are gentle. By wiping chalk vigorously over a corner stamp, the black took on a soft glow. The design on the right between the top and bottom photos is made from the negative pieces of a punch. (The negative pieces are those you usually trash. They create the open holes.) By gluing the negative pieces down in a design, they took on the look of old silhouettes or paper cutting.

TECHNIQUE: *Using a Journaling Stamp*

◄ Stamp the corner stamp on plain archival paper to make four images. (You may wish to do extras for later use or in case of mistakes.) Use the corner template from scrapbookstorytelling.com to draw the flaps you'll fold beneath the photos.

Using a sponge paint bush or a large brush, wipe pastel chalk over the stamped images. If you stamped in black, as I did, you'll notice how the pastel softens the stamped image. Cut out the corner stamps. ►

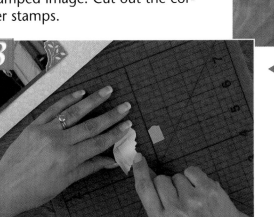

◄ Fold down the sides on the corner stamps and add a photo split to the backs where the two folded flaps meet. Slip the photo into the corner stamps. Press down and make sure the photo splits hold the corner stamp in place. Adjust them if needed. Add more photo splits and put the photo on the page.

Practice stamping with your journaling stamp. Become familiar with its line spacing and use the index on the wooden handle as a guide. Using a permanent marker, draw an arrow on the wooden handle to help you tell which end is up. Ink the stamp and press. Re-ink and press again to add a second set of lines. ►

Journaling Stamps

When I met Karen Greenstreet of Scrapbookin' Stamps at a scrapbook show, I thought, "Finally, a way to combine stamping and journaling. And such fun!"

What to Buy: Every scrapbooker needs at least one journaling stamp to put down simple lines on a page. Start with a simple stamp because you can use it over and over.

Practice: Practice with your stamp so you are familiar with the line spacing. If desired, you might want to use a stamp positioner to help you.

Make Extras: Stamp up a dozen or so journaling boxes of different sizes. You can always trim the boxes in half or trim each side to make them more narrow.

TOOLBOX

SUPPLIES USED

Paper:
Sunflower Spatters
Annette Ward by
Provo Craft

Stamp:
Big Sunflower, © 1994
Hero Arts Rubber
Stamps

Ink:
Archival Inks™ by
Ranger Industries

We'll Be Friends
Forever, © The Boyds
Collection LTP, Li-
censed by InterArt Li-
censing Uptown Rub-
ber Stamps

Chalk:
Decorating Chalks by
Craft-T Products

Pencil:
Berol PrismaColor

? STORY STARTERS

*Journal a moment of
friendship. What were
you doing? Did any-
thing make you laugh?
Or cry?*

We'll be friends Forever

Elaine and I made our first trip to Salt Lake City, the scrapbooking capital of the world in August of 1999. When we saw these wild sunflowers along the road, I had to have a photo.

Notice the beautiful mountains in the distance. When I stepped up to the hill, I heard a funny noise—was it a snake? I hustled off the hill, quickly!

Meet My Forever Friend

Early on, Elaine and I discussed why people don't stay friends. We decided to be "Forever Friends," the kind who work through disagreements. So far, so good. When I saw this paper, its colors matched our Utah photos. Unfortunately, the flowers seemed too small in my pictures. By combining the phrase and a stamp of a sunflower, the headline pulls together the colors, the image and the thought behind this page.

TECHNIQUE: *Using a Phrase Stamp*

◄ First ink and stamp the image of the sunflower on the left side of plain archival paper. Using the index on the back of your phrase stamp as a placement guide, ink and stamp your phrase next to the flower.

Using color pencils and/or markers, ► color in the flower and the bees. Note that the petals in the back should be darker than the ones in the front.

◄ Using a sponge wedge, pick up yellow chalk and rub it across both stamped images. Be sure to take the chalk past the edges of the page title paper. Trim it and adhere it to your page.

It's Just a Phrase She's Going Through

Once in a while, a phrase echoes a chorus in your heart. You look at the words and say, "That's it."

By all means, buy those stamps. You can use phrases over and over. Here's how:

Cards: Phrases make it simple to turn out cards. Keep one as your pattern and stamp to your heart's content.

Backgrounds: Repeat a phrase over and over to create a background. Add art and photos.

Artwork: Separate the phrase and the art. Using the masking technique we shared on the Clover page (see page 7), you can take apart an image and use its components.

Storing Your Stamp Collection

Organization is so personal. What works for one person may only confuse another. After many missteps, this works for me:

Plastic Drawers: Because wooden handled stamps are heavy, a plastic drawer unit with shallow drawers works well. With deep drawers, the weight of the stamps causes the sides of the drawer unit to buckle.

Label Drawers by Topic: You'll see your stamps falling into areas of interest. Labels which might work include plants, animals, food, people, phrases, borders, backgrounds, sets, alphabets, landscapes, hobbies, travel, kid stuff, music, antiques, scenes, cartoons, borders, frames, ethnic, clothes, babies, and holidays.

TOOLBOX

SUPPLIES USED

Paper:
Red with Stars, © 1997
Design Originals

Stamp:
Chuck E Cheese's

Star: Simply Stamps by
Plain Enterprises

Ink:
Dauber Duos by
Tsukineko

Paint:
Delta Paints

Font:
CK Kids

? STORY STARTERS

*Do your children have
a favorite fun spot?
Where do you take
children who visit from
out of town? What do
you do once you are
there?*

Pasqual was a newbie to Chuck E. Cheese, but Michael was an old hand. Sometimes they played together, but eventually Michael got tired of having a "shadow." He also got frustrated when Pasqual refused to listen to him and kept "losing" tokens. Still they had a memorable time. Summer '99

Monkeying Around at the Mouse House

These photos presented a challenge. With so many colors, blinking lights and signage, I needed a method for pulling together the page. First, I cropped close to my subjects to cut clutter. Then, by using Chuck E as a primary image and by repeating two strong colors, red and purple, I brought the images together.

Bright colors evoke a strong emotional response of excitement. Remember that your choice of colors tells your stories on an emotional level.

TECHNIQUE: *Using Foam Stamps*

◀ Use a Dauber Duo to ink the red and purple parts of the foam image. Put ink only on the parts you want. If you make a mistake, you can wipe off some of the ink with a cotton swab. Stamp the images, making more than you need. Use the corner template and proceed as on Womanwriter (see page 29).

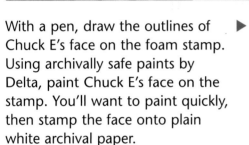

With a pen, draw the outlines of Chuck E's face on the foam stamp. Using archivally safe paints by Delta, paint Chuck E's face on the stamp. You'll want to paint quickly, then stamp the face onto plain white archival paper. ▶

◀ Correct any mistakes and fill in any skimpy spaces with the Delta paint. The paint dries pretty quickly. Once it's dry, you can paint over the top of your first coat. Use a marker to outline the face and to complete the features.

A Stamp by Any Other Name is Still a Stamp

Yes, we put "rubber stamps" on the cover, but golly, isn't this fun, too? Foam stamps are cheap, cute, and simple to stamp. Don't go looking for Chuck E Cheese in your craft store, though. My son won the foam face of the cartoon character with coupons at our local Chuck E Cheese's restaurant.

My point? Look around and be creative. Here are a few household items I've used as "rubber" stamps:

The sole of my house slipper, rubber bands, corks, raw potatoes, erasers, cookie cutters, sponges, toy tires, rags, rubber canning jar rings, fingers, rubber washers (like they put between a nut and a bolt), and corrugated cardboard (paint the ridges).

Delta Dawn

Archivally safe paints by Delta give you tons of new options for customizing pages.

Use Delta paints for the following:

Stenciling: The stenciling aisle of your craft store is overflowing with neat templates you can use on your pages.

Stippling: Grab an old toothbrush, touch the bristles lightly into the paint, and splatter dots of paint all over your page. You can lay down a mask first and leave an open unpainted area if desired.

Stamping: Stamps aren't just for ink. Try them with your Delta paints. The wider the design on the stamp, the better your image will be because the paint is a bit thicker than ink.

SUPPLIES USED

Paper:
Keeping Memories
Alive

Stamp:
Stamps for Journaling
© Scrapbookin' Stamps

Alphabet Rubber
Stamps, © 1998 Hero
Arts Rubber Stamps

Ink:
Memory Acid Free Ink
Pad by Inkadinkado

Punch:
Clover punch
by McGill

*How do you celebrate
holidays? Are there
special dishes you
cook? Tableware you
drag out? Songs
you sing?*

Stamp It Cool, Not Cute

The weather was so gloomy that week in March. I dragged out the St. Patrick's plates, napkins and cookies. Soon we were all smiling. Although the theme of the page is quickly apparent, it isn't cutesy. As my son grows older, stamps help me to make pages that are masculine yet fun.

Note the simple use of the clover punch to create negative space in the journaling mat. This works especially well when punching out a solid paper so that a patterned or contrasting paper shows through.

TECHNIQUE: *Using Alphabet Stamps*

◄ Print your headline on a piece of waste paper. Count the number of letters, spaces and punctuation marks. Divide your total by two. This number is the middle character or letter of your headline. (Even numbers will fall between two characters.)

Cut a paper strip for your headline. ▶ Measure and mark the paper's mid-point. Stamp the middle character of your headline at the mid-point. (If the mid-point is between two letters, stamp one on each side.) Continue stamping, working from the center out. Color in the headline.

◄ Ink and stamp the The Family Times journaling stamp. (You may wish to make several, so you have a few to use on other pages.) Journal on The Family Times. Cut it out and add it to the page.

Know Your ABCs

You'll want as many alphabet stamps as possible. You can mix them, match them or use them for backgrounds.

Center Your Headline

Get comfortable with the counting technique shared here. You'll use it all the time. Don't forget to count punctuation marks and the spaces between letters. You can be even more precise by giving wide letters like W and M two counts and narrow letters like I, T, F and L a half count.

Fill-In Techniques

Outlined alphabet stamps can be customized by coloring the inside of the letters to match your page. Stamp letters in a pale color then...

Color Them In: Start with the lightest shade and color over it or add darker shades. One way to darken color is to cross-hatch your strokes. On your first pass, you might stroke from upper left to lower right. On the second pass, go from upper right to lower left. The result is even and dense color.

Then Re-Outline: Go over your letter outlines with a fairly sharp pencil or a marker as your final step. This tidies up any stray coloring marks.

SUPPLIES USED

Stamps:
Center Stage Frame,
©1997 Posh
Impressions

Classic Alphabet
Rubber Stamp
Collection

Trimmer:
Fiskars

? STORY STARTERS

What are your child's accomplishments in the arts? Show the child's teacher and explain what was required of your child as part of a public performance.

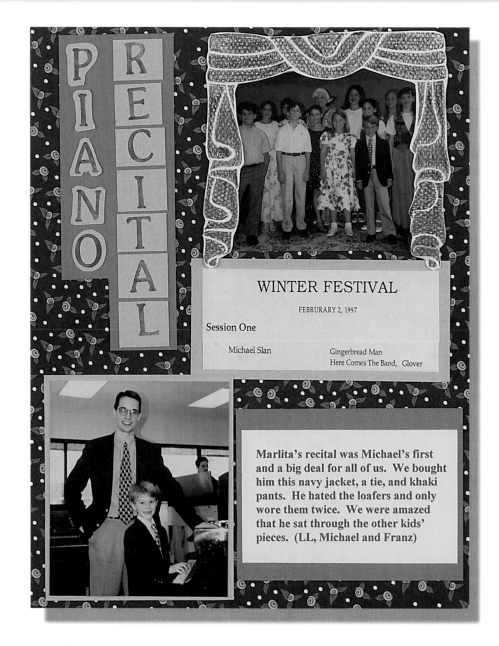

You Don't Have to Draw When You Can Stamp

Draw a curtain? Forget about it! With rubber stamps you don't need to be an accomplished artist to decorate your pages. In fact, lack of artistic skill is probably the number one reason most of us buy stamps.

A curtain stamp like this can be used over and over for new additions, accomplishments, announcements, plays, awards, ceremonies, unveilings, and so on. All in all, it's a stamp virtuoso!

TECHNIQUE: *Creating Tile Lettering*

◄ Ink and stamp the curtain image twice. Use a pencil or marker to add shading and color in any un-inked spots. Cut out both sets of curtains. To make the sides longer, cut the side drapes off one set and adhere them under the side drapes of the other set.

Trim two pieces of paper wide enough to accommodate your letters plus about 1/2" each so you will have an extra 1/4" on each side, right and left. Add HERMAfix to the back of the strip and stick it to your work pad. ▶

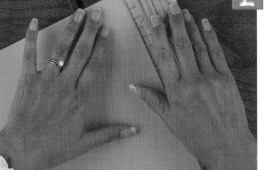

◄ Mark spaces the width of a letter plus about 1/4". Stamp your letters, keeping the letters inside the marked spaces. Trim the letters with a paper cutter into squares or tiles.

Lightly draw around the remaining ▶ letters to leave a small amount of paper as matting. Cut along the pencil lines.

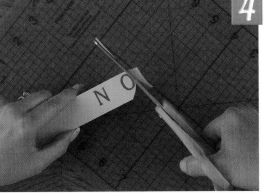

Work Pads and Cutting Mats

Different craft mats protect your desk or table top and help you be more precise in your work.

Fiskars makes a two-sided craft mat with a self-healing side for cutting and a durable working surface on the reverse. At 9" x 12", it's handy for small work.

Scrappin' Basics offers an All Purpose Scrappin' Mat at 14" x 14" that you can cut on. This size is ideal for 12" x 12" pages.

To get crisp stamping impressions, a foam stamping mat works wonders. If you can't find one, try several magazines or newspapers stacked together or a foam-backed plastic kitchen placemat.

TOOLBOX

SUPPLIES USED

Paper:
Plain gray

Stamp:
Gold Leaf Frame,
© StampCraft

Drip Drops, © Posh
Presents, by Rubber
Stampede

Ink:
Memory Acid Free Ink
Pad by Inkadinkado

3-D Crystal Lacquer by
Sakura Hobby Craft

Embossing Powder:
Gold Jewel by E.T.'s
Rubber Stamps

? STORY STARTERS

Are there any sites your family has visited in the spirit of homage? What are they and why did you visit?

Visiting Jim Morrison's Grave

While we were in Paris, Jane asked that we visit Jim
Morrison's grave at the Pere-Lachaise cemetery. We bought
a map, but we didn't need it because all we had to do
was follow the 1 ½ million fans who visit
annually to leave booze, letters and flowers at the site.
Morrison died of a heart attack while
soaking in a tub at age 27.

The drizzle seemed like a
perfect accompaniment to
to the crumbling, spooky
mausoleums where cats hid.

Capturing the Drab of a Drizzle

Most rainy day papers look perfect with photos of kids in bright yellow slickers. But our visit to Pere Lachaise was spooky. As we followed the cobblestone path, a scroungy cat jumped out from inside a crumbling mausoleum. Boy, were we scared!

My goal was to capture the feeling of that gray day and to convey a sense of Paris, where even rock stars seem classy. That's why the frame for the Jim Morrison portrait had to be romantic. I found a perfect frame, but it was too small, so I enlarged it.

TECHNIQUE: *Expanding a Stamp Frame*

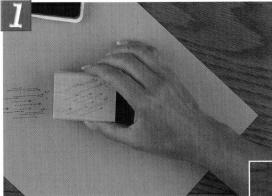

◀ Stamp the background paper by inking the rain stamp and repeating the pattern over the entire page. Start in a corner and work left to right, then move down a row and repeat, slightly overlapping and staggering each imprint.

Stamp the picture frame two times, ▶ using slow drying, waterproof pigment ink.

◀ Generously sprinkle on gold embossing powder. Tap off the excess. Heat to raise the design. Color in the frame with pencils or markers.

Cut the frames apart, following ▶ along one of the designs within the border. Cut out the centers of the frames. You should have "L" shaped pieces and straight pieces. Combine the frames using pieces of both to make the new frame larger. Adhere the pieces and cover them with crystal lacquer.

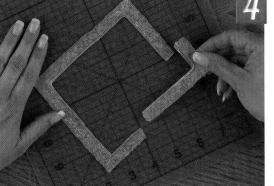

Camouflage

You can cut apart about anything and conceal the cut edges if you follow these tips:

1. Work only with patterns. On solids, the two edges will usually show.

2. Cut along a pattern. The eye follows the pattern and ignores the cut edge.

3. Make the cut as irregular as possible. That is, a cut with deckle edge scissors will blend in much more easily than with straight edge scissors.

Be a student of nature. The irregular dappled spots on fawns help them blend into their surroundings. So do the uneven markings on toads. Once you learn this trick, you'll combine all sorts of images and no one will know the difference.

? STORY STARTERS

Document a child's growing understanding of the world around him or her. Note how the child learns to have an impact on the environment.

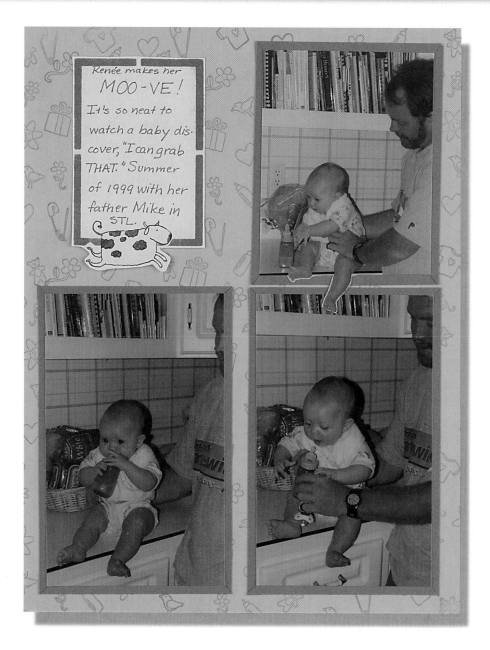

Stamps Make Matching Colors Easy

Maybe pink and turquoise paper floods the racks in your scrapbook store, but mine was all out. Once again, my trusty stamps created the background and the journaling box to emphasize my photos.

Notice the way Renee's chubby little leg and foot hang out of the picture on the top right. This is an example of a bump crop. Draw an imaginary frame around your photo. What sticks out beyond that frame? Cut around it and leave the part of the image sticking out for a more interesting photo.

TECHNIQUE: *Masking to Add a Stencil Border*

Ink your stamp and begin stamping at the upper left hand corner. While the stamp is on the paper, use a pencil to make a tick (a faint mark) on the right side of the stamp and on the bottom. Use these marks to help you line up the stamp for your next image, to the right of your first image.

Stamp the cow image on waste paper. Cut around it. Since this is for a mask, you only need to cut the right and left sides closely. Now, ink only the cow (ignore other parts of the stamp) and stamp it again on archival paper, leaving lots of room around the cow.

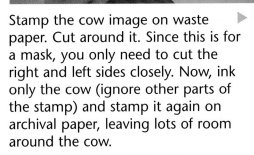

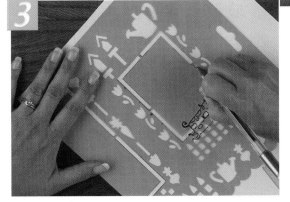

Cover your cow with the cow mask. Lay the box stencil so that it abuts the right and left side of the cow. Use a marker to color in the box stencil. Lift the stencil straight up. Let the ink dry and then remove the cow mask. Cut out the box and adhere it to your page.

Classic Masking

This is the technique most people mean when they talk about masking a stamp. Here, we've used masking so you can be a sloppy colorer and get right next to your cow.

Usually, you'll mask one stamp so you can stamp the paper again and not destroy that first image.

Masking can be confusing, so try this memory aid: Mask what you want to protect—like the Lone Ranger masks his identity. Still confused? Practice on waste paper and then stamp your images on archivally safe paper. It may help to practice by using different colors of ink so you can see what you've done.

Basic Stenciling Techniques

You can be a stenciling whiz in four easy steps:

Mask It—Cover any parts of the stencil you don't want to use with a Post-it Note or masking tape.

Position It—Tack your stencil down. HERMAfix on the back works, but so do the stencil sticker-downers they sell in craft stores.

Ink It—Dab a sponge with rounded edges onto your ink pad. You want the sponge as dry as possible or the ink will run. Sponge a paper towel once. Now lightly sponge your stencil. Repeat until you get the coverage and color you want. (Use a rounded edge sponge because a crisp, straight edge will leave an ink line.)

Lift It—Lift your stencil straight up from the paper. If you wiggle it, the ink may smear.

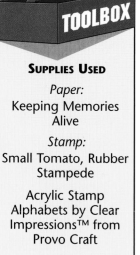

TOOLBOX

SUPPLIES USED

Paper:
Keeping Memories
Alive

Stamp:
Small Tomato, Rubber
Stampede

Acrylic Stamp
Alphabets by Clear
Impressions™ from
Provo Craft

Ink:
Stampin' Up

Pencils:
Berol

STORY STARTERS

Capture a family story. What misconception lead to a chuckle that you never tire of sharing?

One day when Lexie was in grade school (around 1980 or so) she came home and announced to her mother, "Today we had a TOMATO drill." It took Jane a while to figure out that Lexie meant a TORNADO drill. Isn't she the cutest thing in this pretty dress?

Portrait of a Young Lady with a Tomato

I looked for a tomato stamp for months and couldn't find anything I liked. I wanted a realistic looking fruit, and I needed to color it to match the colors in Lexie's dress. Finally, I found this stamp.

By adding a touch of magenta in the deepest shadows, I created a color that didn't clash with her outfit. The clear lettering stamps are a perfect headline size and quite versatile. See how different they look on page 48.

TECHNIQUE: *Using Clear Stamps*

◀ Ink your rubber stamp and stamp it onto archival paper. Use pencils or markers to color in the image. Cut out the image. Use a craft knife to cut the area inside the stems.

Slip one letter from your clear stamp alphabet set into the stamp handle. Ink the stamp and practice stamping. Stamp your image on archival paper. If desired, go over the outline of the letter with a marker. ▶

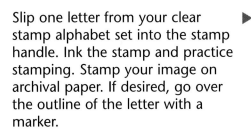

◀ Stamp your journaling stamp on archival paper. Using the index as a guide, line up the stamp and repeat it to make a larger journaling area.

Making the Invisible Visible

Since these stamps are almost transparent, and since they have no index, it can be really difficult to figure out which stamp is which. As soon as you get your stamps, stamp them with black archival ink and then clean them. The archival ink will stain the die making it easy for you to see the image.

Practice

Seeing through stamps makes it much, much easier to position them exactly where you want them. But, the clear stamps that use handles can be a tad difficult to master. Practice will help you achieve a good, precise outline.

Cleaning Your Stamps

My favorite cleaning tool is a stamp cleaning pad by Stampin' Up. (Similar pads can be found in your local craft stores.) In the top third of the pad, squirt some window cleaner **without alcohol**. Add a little water at the top third and let it run into the middle third by tilting the pad. Leave the bottom third as dry as possible. Clean your stamps by stroking them from the window cleaner third to the dry third. Blot them on paper towels or cotton rags.

TOOLBOX

SUPPLIES USED

Paper:
Paper Pizazz

Stamp:
Stamps for Journaling,
© Scrapbookin' Stamps

Ink:
Dauber Duos by
Tsukineko

Marker:
Zig

Pencil:
Berol Prismacolor

? STORY STARTERS

Notice how the children in our lives try to copy what we do. What are your little ones eager to take part in? How will you introduce a new interest to them?

Daniele' T.

January 2000

She brought over

her new Barbie camera to try on us.

ShutterBug

Seeing her mom and me snap so many photos, Daniele' asked, "Can't I have a camera?" So Elaine bought her a Barbie model. The best feature? The camera even stores a small hair comb so the photographer can "spruce up." It's not often that Daniele' gets to visit without her brother or Michael. She loved it.

A Camera in Basic Pink Makes a Fashion Statement

My die cut collection had cameras in basic black, but the ever fashion forward Miss Daniele was holding a Barbie camera in basic pink. The colors had to be girly, but because Daniele was wearing a patriotic sweater, blue needed to be brought along for balance. The Scrapbookin' Stamps journaling stamp of a camera gave me color flexibility. Notice that Daniele's mom Elaine is cropped (slightly cut off). Your mind fills in the rest of Elaine's body. Tight crops help emphasize your focal point.

TECHNIQUE: *Combining Journaling & Frame Stamps*

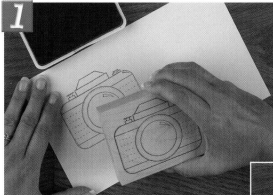

◀ Stamp the image on archival paper using a pigment ink. Let it dry slightly. Lightly dust the image with embossing powder. Emboss using a heat gun. Journal on the stamped image. Cut out the center. Affix the photo beneath the hole.

Stamp your large journaling area by repeatedly stamping your journaling lines. ▶

◀ Lightly trace in the letters of your headline, overlapping and letting the letters go up and down. Use a light pink pencil. If you like your results, color in the letters and re-outline them with a marker. Then cut out the headline. Use a craft knife to trim out the letter centers.

A Mixed Color Embossing Job

If you decide you don't want an opaque embossing area, try this: Let your pigment ink dry slightly. Tap on a small amount of embossing powder. (You can even use a bristle paint brush to brush off some of the powder.) Tap off any extra. Now heat with your embossing gun.

All of the Trimmings

Don't waste your time carefully trimming the photo behind the hole in the camera. Center the photo. Attach the photo. Flip it over and trim only what sticks out and shows from the front. No need to be neat about it.

Stamp from Light to Dark

Train yourself to always stamp from light colors to dark colors. If you stamped this camera first in light pink, and you decided it was too light, you could always add embossing powder, as I did, or stamp over the image with darker ink or use a marker to touch up the lines. You can even wipe the stamp on a paper towel and re-ink it without cleaning the die. But if you stamp with a dark ink, you have fewer choices and you must completely clean your stamp to re-ink it in a lighter color or the dark ink will mess up the lighter ink source.

SUPPLIES USED

Paper:
Crowns: Rueger
Checks: MM Colors
By Design

Stamps:
Stamps for Journaling,
© Scrapbookin' Stamps

Alphabet Rubber
Stamps by Hero Arts

Do It Yourself by
Stamp Affair

Ink:
Archival Inks by
Ranger Industries

Marker:
Zig

? STORY STARTERS

Journal the addition of a new pet. How does your family interact with this new creature? Document the pet's initial size.

Capture the Elegance of Royalty with Classy Embellishments

Since my son is positive he's a prince, it's only natural that his pet rat expected to be treated like a blue blood, too. When I set these photos on the paper with the crowns, the images of the rat and the Legos castle were overwhelmed. Instead, a thin strip of the crowns became a one-sided border. Stamps gave me the freedom to embellish the page with matching colors, mood and theme. A crown enlarged on my photocopier was used as a pattern for the large crown by the page title.

TECHNIQUE: *Aligning Lettering with a Guide*

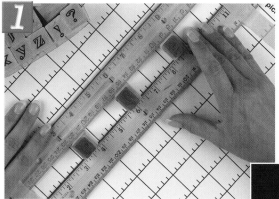

◄ Set three rubber stamps handle-side down in a line across your craft mat. Snuggle one ruler on top of the stamps and one below the stamps. Use masking tape to tape down the extreme left and right ends of your rulers. You should now have a channel to guide your stamps in a straight line.

Slip your paper under the rulers, lining up the left edge with a grid line. ► Starting from left to right, stamp your headline. Use the up and down grid and the marks on the ruler to help you space your letters evenly. When finished, slip out your paper. Color your headline and trim it.

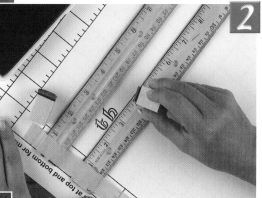

◄ Stamp your "thought bubble" stamp on archival paper. Repeat three times. Journal inside the "thought bubbles." Trim.

Gridlock Makes It Easy

Stamping letters in a straight line was too complicated for me. This grid system works like a charm. If you use bigger or smaller stamps, just undo the tape and readjust the width between your rulers.

The large Scrappin' Basics mat works especially well for this grid because it is 14" x 14," and you can tape down your ruler with space to spare.

Crooked Letters?

If you do stamp letters and find them too crooked to use, cut them apart and turn them into tile letters as I did with the Houdini headline.

About that "Houdini" Headline

I found a rubber stamp kit on sale at a scrapbooking store. The kit advertised that all the letters of the alphabet were inside, plus a wooden handle. You were supposed to attach the letters of your name to the handle. Ha! No way was I going to waste an entire alphabet. At my local hardware store, I had the 1/2" diameter dowels cut into short dowels about six inches long. I adhered the letters to the 1/2" square end using the rest of the dowel as a handle. I wrote the letter name on the opposite 1/2" end to use as an index. For about $6 in wood and $6 in stamps I put together an entire 1/2" alphabet.

?STORY STARTERS

Follow your family outside to record interactions with the weather. Include how kids find ways to play with each other and their surroundings.

TOOLBOX

SUPPLIES USED

Paper: The Paper Patch

Stamps: Snowman: Stamps for Journaling, © Scrapbookin' Stamps
Letter: Acrylic Stamp Alphabets with a Clear View™, Provo Craft

The Thrill of the Hill

We live in a hilly subdivision, and our back lawn is a steep slope. Michael's friend Kip Loynd had spent the night, and the boys awoke to a blanket of wet, slippery snow. My challenge with this page was staying true to little boys everywhere. The images had to be masculine and bright. But, a lot of snowy paper and embellishments are blue or holiday themed. By being able to repeat the colors of the photograph in the background paper, the snowman's hat and the headline, I found the look I wanted—all boy.

TECHNIQUE: *Using a Three-Part Stamp*

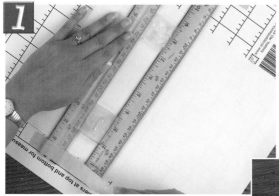

◀ Adjust the width on your grid, as explained on page 47. Since the clear stamps are soft, make sure to use the stamp handle for sizing your channel. Slip a piece of paper under the grid. Stamp your headline, color it in with markers and trim around the pieces.

On a piece of archival paper, separately stamp all three portions of your journaling snowman. Color in the details as desired. Cut out the pieces. Use photo safe tape on the backside to join the pieces. ▶

◀ Stamp "thought bubbles" on archival paper. Journal on the image. Cut the image out and trim off the small bubbles at the bottom.

Do These Letters Look Familiar?

This is the same alphabet style as used on the Tomato Drill headline on page 42. Notice the big difference made by coloring in the design.

Of course, there's a third way to use these letters, and that is to color them in with a solid color that matches the outline.

Snip, Snip Here; Snip, Snip There

Yep, I simply chopped off the little bubbles of the "thought bubble." I decided to use the "thought bubble" as a caption rather than a comment. Experiment with your stamps. Stamp them on waste paper and use your scissors. It's just one more way to get your money's worth.

Mark It Up. Using Markers to Ink Stamps

If you're already a scrapbooker, you probably have a selection of markers. They work fine to ink your stamps, as long as you aren't trying to ink a big, solid area. There are two kinds of markers, however, and you'll want to be sure you know what you're using.

Waterproof—Once these are down, you can color over them or use watercolor pencils and the ink won't run.

Water-Base—The ink of these markers can run, which makes them perfect for blending or using watercolor techniques. If you stamp an outline in this ink, it may smear or change when you color over it.

TOOLBOX

SUPPLIES USED

Paper:
© Shelley Hely

Stamp:

Li'l Kitty by Rubber Stampede

Miracle, © Running Rhino & Co. by Up-town Rubber Stamps

Ink:
Dauber Duos by Tsukineko

Pencils:
Derwent Watercolour

Pens:
Marvy

? STORY STARTERS

Note those creatures or situations that have a particular attraction for your child. Does she stop to stare at dogs? Note the attraction AND the response.

When Michael was 22 months old, we visited Paris. He saw this cat through the window and wanted to love the kitty. Even though they were separated by glass and a language barrier, Michael and the cat both spoke the language of friendship.

Spring 1991

How Much is that Kitty in the Window?

You can't really tell from the photos, at least not at first glance, but the cat and Michael were separated by a display window. My challenge was to make it more clear what was happening. So I decided to repeat the interaction, using stamps to illustrate the story. It took a while to find the right cat stamp, but when I spotted this little meow-meister, he was the one.

TECHNIQUE: *Stamping on Vellum*

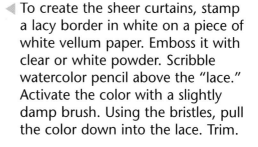

◁ To create the sheer curtains, stamp a lacy border in white on a piece of white vellum paper. Emboss it with clear or white powder. Scribble watercolor pencil above the "lace." Activate the color with a slightly damp brush. Using the bristles, pull the color down into the lace. Trim.

To create the window frame, stamp ▷ your image and color in the frame. Cut out the center of the frame. Adhere the curtain about 2/3 of the way down the window. Attach it to the back of the window frame with photo-safe tape. Trim the curtain.

◁ Stamp the cat with a water-base ink. Lightly color in the cat and collar with watercolor pencils. Dampen a paintbrush. Starting at the outside edge of the outline, pull it in with the damp brush to activate the color. Activate the colors on the collar.

To create the headline, ink only the ▷ leaves of the frame. Stamp leaves over and over in a random fashion. Put the letter template over the random stamping. Use a marker to outline the letters. Color in the leaves in the letters. Cut out the letters and attach them to the mat.

Tip!

More Than Meets the Eye

If you don't celebrate Hannukah, you might walk right past this lovely stamp. That would be a shame. See if you can find the following images within the stamp by looking at the imprint of the total stamp in Box 2:

• Menorah or candelabra

• single candle in candle holder

• single candle

• candles in a row like on a birthday cake

• frame

• leaves

• single frame (only print the outside or the inside double-lined box)

• double frame (make the inside solid by coloring over the leaves)

• tree with leaves (use the candelabra and print leaves instead of candles on top of the candelabra arms)

SUPPLIES USED

Paper:
Paper Pizazz

Stamps:
Earth: © 1991 All Night
Media

Airplane: Travel Stamps
by Hero Arts

Alphabet: by
CraftsMate

Stickers:
Mrs. Grossman's
Design Lines

Markers:
Zig

Pigma Micron by
Sakura

Chalks:
Decorating Chalks
by Craft-T Products

What was the first signage that announced you had reached your destination? Be sure to photograph it.

Olivia and Bill left St. Louis for Germany on October 1, 1999. They arrived in Munich the 2nd.

Up, Up and Away as They Fly the Friendly Skies

While playing the computer game "Where in the World is Carmen Sandiego?" with my son, the image of the plane taking off and buzzing around the world really stuck in my mind.

I put together the world and the plane and drew in the motion lines. Then I streaked chalk across the paper. Finally, the Mrs. Grossman's Design Lines made a crisp border. The page title was cleared for take-off and landed on this page with my pal, Olivia and her hubby, Bill.

TECHNIQUE: *Combining Images to Make a Page Title*

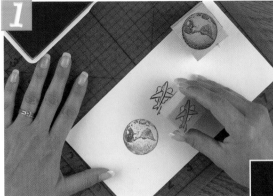

◀ Cut a piece of paper to the size you want for a page topper. Stamp the world and the plane.

Stamp the word "TRAVEL." Note that you don't have to line up the letters. Color in the letters and the images. Add motion lines around the globe. Outline the letters in black. ▶

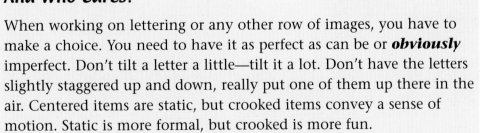

◀ Add streaks of chalk using a cosmetic sponge as an applicator. Add Design Lines. Retouch the chalk if needed.

Just How Crooked is Crooked? And Who Cares?

When working on lettering or any other row of images, you have to make a choice. You need to have it as perfect as can be or **obviously** imperfect. Don't tilt a letter a little—tilt it a lot. Don't have the letters slightly staggered up and down, really put one of them up there in the air. Centered items are static, but crooked items convey a sense of motion. Static is more formal, but crooked is more fun.

And here's a tip I learned from my sister Margaret, the art teacher: It's not a mistake; it's a design element. Too many folks toss stuff out too quickly. If it isn't exactly as you planned, work with it. See what you can do with your design before you give up. Even if you don't keep the finished product, you'll probably learn something.

Tip!

Laying It on the Line

One type of sticker I buy every time I shop is the Mrs. Grossman's Design Lines. They easily make a perfect, clean border.

Here's a way to get the Design Lines down straight:

1. Put one end of the tape down where you want the line to start.

2. Holding that first end down, gently stretch the tape to where you want the line to end.

3. Press down the end, holding the tape taut. This is what makes the tape go on straight.

4. Press down the center of the tape.

5. Smooth down the areas in between.

6. Trim off the ends.

Again, the trick is keeping the tape taut while going from the starting point to the end.

STORY STARTERS

Is there a special place your family has returned to for years? What draws you to that place? What discoveries have you made?

Sometimes It All Comes Together, and Sometimes It all Falls Apart. Or, How NOT to Hold a Starfish

Right as I snapped this photo, the starfish's arm snapped off. UGGGH. Lucky for the sea creature, it will grow back. This is a page where all the elements came together: the Old Navy shirt, the grey of the sand, the misty photo, and the plover stamp. As I travel, I visit stamp stores all around the country. Rubber stamps make great souvenirs and often a local vendor will have stamps germane to that area that you won't find at home.

TECHNIQUE: *Creating a Border with a Single Stamp*

◀ Stamp the letters of the headline. Color in the letters with a marker.

Mix chalk colors on the tip of a cosmetic or a stamping sponge. Apply the colors in a wave design. Make sure the chalk color extends off the left side of your paper. ▶

◀ Stamp the phrase in navy ink. Using the index as a guide, stamp the birds in black next to the phrase. Color in both stamps. Use a small point marker (such as a Micron .01) to extend the top line of the sand dunes and add the detail. Add chalk to the background and to the sand.

Put waste paper under the page. Begin stamping a row of seashells so that the stamp is half on and half off the left edge of the paper. Make a pencil tick at the far right end of the stamp handle. Use the pencil tick to help you line up the stamp to the right of your first image. Stamp and repeat, going off the right edge with the image. ▶

Off the Edge and Over the Top

By printing your stamp off the left and right edges, you get what professionals call a "bleed." The image extends into an imaginary space. The converse of a bleed is a border. A border frames a space and acts as a visual organizer. A bleed extends a space and makes our mind fill in the infinity beyond the image.

Since the ocean under the words "Life at Sea" bleeds off the page, this border makes a nice counterbalance. Look for bleeds and borders in art. Both styles have their uses.

Mike, Mom and Kevin go on an

EXPLORE!

We walked through the brush to the creek. Our "catch" for the day was 8 frogs, a big crayfish, 5 fish, and one tick. YUCK!

June 1999

TOOLBOX

SUPPLIES USED

Paper:
Cream with green speckles

Stamp:
Jar, © Inkadinkado

Stamp-A-Scene, ©Posh Impressions, from Rubber Stampede

Pens:
Metallic Gel Rollers by Marvy

Marker:
Zig

? STORY STARTERS

Is there something your child begs you to do again and again? Journal about a favorite activity you share.

Amphibian Adoption Unit Mobile 1, Can You Hear Me?

*I*f it hops, slithers, runs or jumps, it's probably coming home with us. Using vellum helped me make the jar seem real. Although I had paper patterned with grass, its green was too intense, and the pre-printed paper overwhelmed my photos. I decided to make my own grassy knoll.

These landscape stamps came in a kit, which made them a great buy. And, the selection made it easy since I didn't have to think about what sort of rocks and plants I might need to be semi-realistic.

TECHNIQUES: *Creating a Landscape & Glass Jar*

◄ On archival white paper, stamp the jar. Add a frog to the inside of the jar using a sticker or a stamp. Color in the frog stamp and the jar lid.

On white vellum, stamp the jar in black. Color in the lid with a gold metallic pen. Cut out the vellum jar. Add HERMAfix dots behind the lid. Attach the vellum jar over the archival jar, matching lid to lid. Cut out both jars. ▶

◄ Stamp the landscape background. Use multiple colors of green ink, starting with lighter greens first. Stamp in the rocks.

Cut out around the top of a clump ▶ of grass. Slip a matted photo under a clump of grass so that the stamped grass actually extends over the photo. Add photo splits to the back to secure the photo to the page.

Stamping Off

Stamping off is a way to get a fainter version of your stamped image. You "stamp off" by stamping your image twice or more, not pausing to re-ink your die before your second stamping.

For texture and color variation, stamping off works well. By stamping a second image, you get two shades, a dark and a light one from your ink.

You can also use stamping off to make a softer version of any color. Plus, you can create the illusion of motion by continuing to stamp off until you are out of ink.

TOOLBOX

SUPPLIES USED

Paper:
Paper Pizazz

Pens:
Heart Stamper Pen by
Pentech

Roller Pen: Z-Rollz by
Inventure

? STORY STARTERS

How do you feel about your car? Many people have pet names for their automobiles and ascribe personalities to them. Tell about your vehicular relationship.

I had been driving a broken-down older car for five years when my husband surprised me with this used *BMW* convertible as an anniversary gift. When my son and his friend saw the car, they decided I had to drive them to school the next day. The morning dawned cold, cold, cold. I bundled the boys in blankets and took them to school.

By the time we got to the school, the boys were frozen!

Backgrounds Made Simple Using Stamping Techniques

*T*he photo at the bottom right of the page above was problematic. There was so much going on in the background that you couldn't see the car or me for the trees. Cutting away the background is called a silhouette crop. That's what I did here, leaving myself with a new problem: What do I put behind this photo? The background paper wouldn't work because the lips were too big and prominent. I decided to create a new background for my photo by using stamps.

TECHNIQUE: *Using Roller Stamps & Stamping Markers*

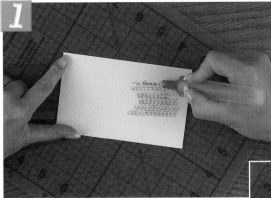

◀ Create background paper by rolling your roller stamp back and forth across white paper. (The ink is already in the pen.) Slightly overlap the lines. Cut your background paper into two pieces.

Finish one piece of the background ▶ paper by adding hearts stamped with your stamping marker. (Again, the ink is already in the pen.) Space the hearts randomly across the paper.

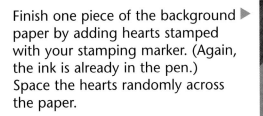

◀ Place your letter template over the background paper with hearts and outline the letters of your headline. Cut out the letters. Use a craft knife on the centers. Adhere the letters to the pink lips die cut.

Affix your silhouette cropped photo to a piece of the background paper with solid hearts on it. Trim the photo and the background and mat them. Add them to your page.

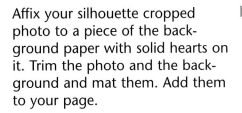

Hey, These Aren't Rubber Stamps Either

Maybe not, but I checked with one manufacturer and found out their ink is close enough to pH neutral to make their pens safe.

Roller pens don't always roll in a straight line so you might want to "road test" your wheels in the office supply store before making a purchase.

This is just another example of how inexpensively you can use stamped images to customize your pages. I bought a box of the stamping markers and had a whale of a time playing with them.

While I featured a car, this page would work for Valentine's Day, or any other special time.

TOOLBOX

SUPPLIES USED

Paper:
Plain blue

Stamps:
Stamp-A-Scene, ©
Posh Impressions, from
Rubber Stampede

Classic Alphabet
Rubber Stamp
Collection, ©
Inkadinkado

Ink:
ColorBox Pigment
Brush Pads

? STORY STARTERS

What prehistoric sites have you visited? What can you discover about their history?

While visiting Grandma Marge in Vincennes, Michael and I decided to take a quick side trip to Sonotabac Prehistoric Indian Mound, which is less than 5 miles from her house. We climbed the steep hill only to find stone steps running down the backside. Little is known about how or why the mounds were built, but archeologists believe they were built from about 1000 BC to 1500 AD by many different Indian societies. This mound is probably a burial mound from the Adena culture which inhabited the central Ohio Valley.

SONOTABAC

Whew, That Mound was Big!

I wanted a way to show the proportions of the mound in comparison with Michael. I took a photo of the entire mound and used it as a pattern. On my photocopier, I enlarged the mound photo until this photo of Mike climbing perfectly matched (size-wise) the same area of the photocopy. Then I used the photocopy to guide me as I cut the mound out of grass patterned paper. I added the sign and stamped in the trees and bushes.

TECHNIQUE: *Using Stamps with Paper Piecing*

◀ Trim your grass paper to the desired shape. Use deckle scissors along the top to simulate grass.

Tap a round sponge onto a pad of ▶ white ink. Stamp off the extra ink. Lightly stamp the sponge onto blue paper to look like clouds. Using a light green pencil, lightly trace the top of the green hill onto your blue paper.

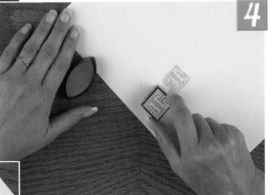

◀ Using a photo of the landscape, stamp in plants and trees. Use the stamping off technique and also stamp the images in black to give the illusion of being distant.

For the journaling box background: ▶ Stamp the petroglyph in light green to create background paper for computer type.

For page title: Stamp light green petroglyphs again in a row, with spaces between each image.

◀ Center and stamp solid letters in dark green on top of the light green petroglyphs. Cut apart the letters and the tiles (squares) and arrange them to form a page title.

Tip!

Printing Computer Type Over Your Stamping

It seems counter-intuitive to stamp first and then print out your journaling on top of your stamping, BUT the ink in most ink jet printers is water soluble. So, if you stamp OVER the computer printing, you may smear it.

Tip!

White Clouds, An Easy Technique

Using the sponge with white ink is as simple as it gets for making clouds in the sky. For more defined clouds, add more ink.

TOOLBOX

SUPPLIES USED

Paper:
The Paper Patch

Stamp:
Circle: Pencil eraser

Ink:
Dauber Duos by
Tsukineko

Pen:
Avery

Stickers:
Mrs. Grossman's
Design Lines

Font:
URW Wood TypeD

Scissors:
Paper Adventures

Punches:
Hand: McGill

Bow and Flowers:
Family Treasures

? STORY STARTERS

Ask your family to tell you what they enjoyed most about the event you're scrapbooking.

SHRINE MOOLAH CIRCUS

We got great tickets from KMOX so Margaret, Michael, Katigan, Makenna, David and I went to the circus. Margaret suggested we go early, and that was a smart idea.

Under the Big Top, Just Clowning Around

Wow, the colors that clowns wear are strong. Because I used a flash, the photo of Michael and his friends came out wonderfully well and very high-contrast. But where to find a clown of the right size, colors and shape? Hmmmm. Time to be creative. Notice how the clown embellishment frames the photo with its body. Because the clown is cropped, you mentally absorb his image, but he doesn't take up all the space on the page. With white on the live clowns' faces and white on the clown embellishment, a white journaling box doesn't look out of place.

TECHNIQUE: *Stamping with a Pencil Eraser*

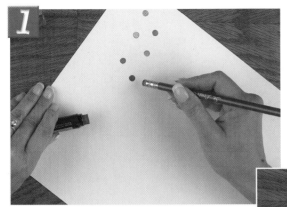

1 ◀ Ink a fresh pencil eraser with the lightest color of your Dauber Duo. Press straight down onto the paper, randomly. Repeat. Wipe off the eraser. Change to another color and repeat until the space is filled.

Photocopy and enlarge the page ▶ or use the clown template from www.scrapbookstorytelling.com to cut out the clown's body and clothes and assemble them. Use a Design Line for his belt.

2

3

◀ Start the clown's face by lightly marking the pattern with colored pencils on white paper. Use foam stamps for hair. Use a Dauber Duo tip for the nose. Use a pencil eraser for cheeks. Use a fine tip Micron pen for the features.

Stamp the foam hat on white ▶ paper. Add the stamp of a star on top, or use a star punch to create a star shape out of yellow paper, if desired. Cut out the hat and affix it to the clown's hair. Affix all pieces and add them to the page.

Stamp balloons in various colors. ▶

4

5

◀ Cut out the balloons. Affix them to the page. On the wrong side of the paper, directly behind the balloons, reinforce the paper with photo safe tape. Thread a needle with white thread. Use the needle to pierce the paper at the end of the balloons. Pull the thread through the paper and around the balloons' ends. Wrap the thread ends around the clown's hand.

TOOLBOX

SUPPLIES USED

Stamps:
Fence: © Rubber Stamps of America

Cloud: Stamp-A-Scene, ©Posh Impressions, from Rubber Stampede

Tree: © 1998 Stampa Rosa

Ink:
ColorBox

Lettering:
Frances Meyer

Scissors:
Paper Adventures

Stencil:
Dot Letters Stencil by Frances Meyer

Other:
Post-it Notes

STORY STARTERS

Why stop with a picture of only your child? Get the neighborhood kids involved. Pay particular attention to the costumes since trends change each year.

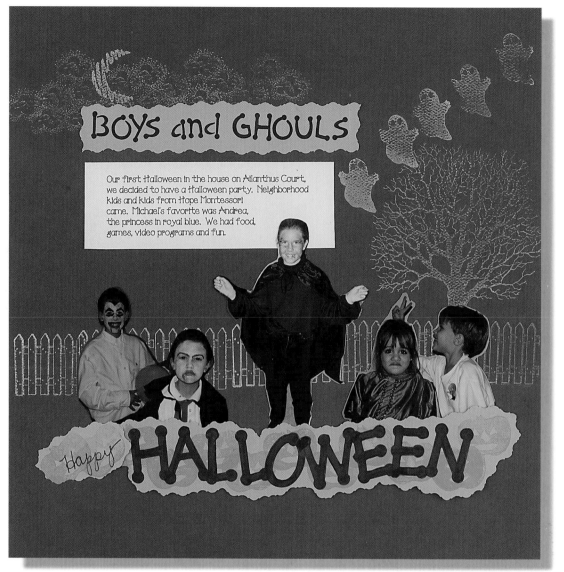

BOYS and GHOULS

Our first Halloween in the house on Ailanthus Court, we decided to have a Halloween party. Neighborhood kids and kids from Hope Montessori came. Michael's favorite was Andrea, the princess in royal blue. We had food, games, video programs and fun.

Happy HALLOWEEN

Dark Paper, Light Ink—What a Treat, Don't You Think?

Some pages owe their style to simple curiosity. What would it look like to use white ink on dark paper, I wondered. About that time, I cleaned the junk drawer and found these Halloween erasers. After intense negotiations with my son (during which he got the better end of the deal, I'm sure), I had two new stamps. One problem you often see with holiday pages is that the paper overwhelms the photos. Keeping background images simple and in one color keeps the spotlight—or the moonlight—on your photos.

TECHNIQUE: *Advanced Masking Techniques*

◀ Ink the fence stamp and stamp it on the page, starting from right to left, making a white pencil tick next to the handle to help you line up your stamp for the next impression. Repeat until you have stamped the fence across the page.

Ink the ghost stamp and make the ▶ impression, then stamp the impression again and again to make the ghost look fainter. Stamp the moon and add clouds by stamping over the moon.

◀ Stamp masks of two ghosts and the fence with colored ink on waste paper. Cut them out. Adhere the masks with HERMAfix to the first and second ghosts and the second stamping of the fence. Stamp the tree in white ink over the masks. Remove the masks.

On tan paper, stamp off an orange ▶ pumpkin and add a fainter image repeatedly.

◀ Position the lettering template over the stamped pumpkins and use a marker to color in the letters that make the headline. Trim around the headline and add it to the page.

Stamping with Kids' Erasers? Yes! It's Fun!

Plus you may even have a few erasers lying around the house that you can use. Attach the eraser with rubber cement to a plastic box, like a candy box, or to the type of boxes that hold paper punches. (The rubber cement won't hold it forever, but you will be able to get some stamping done.)

Save $$ and Spend It on Bigger, Better Stamps

The best reason for being frugal is to have more money to spend on more stamps. Large stamps can be expensive so use coupons when possible, buy from a store that offers a discount to frequent buyers, or save money by buying simple erasers—like this ghost and pumpkin—and use the savings to buy more elaborate stamps like the tree.

TOOLBOX

SUPPLIES USED

Paper:
Paper Pizazz

Stamps:
Alphabet by Clear Stamp

Border stamps, © Judith, Stamps by Judith

Ink:
ColorBox Pigment Brush Pad

Pencil:
Berol

? STORY STARTERS

Who's new in your life? How did he or she find a place in your heart? What is the reaction of your child?

What a Contrast: He's Confident, She's Concerned

You can almost hear her thinking, "Is he licensed to hold babies?" Well, after getting an A in Family Life class, Mike was one confident dude. Whenever Eliza comes to visit, he can't wait to hold her. It's a joy to see my son caring for a younger child. I wanted this page to focus on the photo since their faces are so expressive. The reddish mat picks up the flowers in Eliza's dress. The background paper is figured, but not too fussy. A border of flowers seemed the perfect way to help focus on the children while tying the paper and Eliza's dress together.

TECHNIQUE: *Using Interactive Stamps*

◀ Using your photo as a guide, trace a light pencil line around the picture. This will serve as a guide for stamping a frame.

Stamp the branches on the line, working your way around the frame. Stamp off and also use fresh ink. Add red dots to fill the spaces. Add yellow flowers. Cut along the outside border. Add a matted photo. ▶

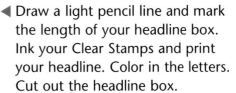

◀ Draw a light pencil line and mark the length of your headline box. Ink your Clear Stamps and print your headline. Color in the letters. Cut out the headline box.

Saving the Best for Last...

This alphabet by Clear Stamps is my favorite, bar none. The stamps are extra squishy so the images are easy to put on paper. The open area in the letters makes it simple to customize your title with color.

The style is so neutral, it goes with almost every theme. The size is perfect for almost any multiple word headline. If you are going to buy just one alphabet set, this is the one to get. Make sure to use archival black ink on it first, so you can tell which letter is which.

How Interactive Stamps Work

Many stamps you see in stores offer a complete image. Interactive stamps can be complete but more often they are designed to work with other stamps so you have more control over your finished image. For example, instead of a wreath stamp, you might use interactive stamps of branches, berries and bows to create your own wreath design. Judith Kleinschmidt is the queen of interactive stamps. You can find her stamps in stamp retail shops under the name "Stamps by Judith." Be sure to ask your retailer for Judith's green sheets that show you how to use her stamps together. The sheets are loaded with great ideas.

TOOLBOX

SUPPLIES USED

Gingham Paper:
Paper Adventures

Stamps:
Rollagraph® Roller Stamp System

Do It Yourself by Stamp Affair

Tiny Backgrounds by Hero Arts

Dot Alphabet and Classic Alphabet by Inkadinkado

Play & Learn Stamp Letter Set by CraftsMate

Alphabet Rubber Stamps by Hero Arts

Ink:
Stampin' Up

ColorBox Pigment Stamp Pad

Imprintz

Archival Inks by Ranger Industries

Pencil
Berol

Marker:
Zig

Letter Stencil:
Frances Meyer

A Letter By Any Other Name is a Design Element

Expand the way you think of letters. Often scrapbookers get into a rut and make very utilitarian headlines. That's fine, especially if your page has a lot going on and you want to keep the headline simple. But, take time to play. The more you experiment, the better you'll get at stamping. Ever season a cast-iron skillet? Stamps seem to need a similar treatment. They really don't give you their best image until you've used them a couple of times.

TECHNIQUE: *Getting Creative with Letters*

Draw a wavy line with a light pencil. Stamp the letters along the top of the line, leaving space between the words. Go back and draw dots between the words. Stamp a piano at one end. Glue on punch art music notes as shown.

Ink the branches in light pink. Stamp randomly. Clean the stamp and ink the branches in light blue. Stamp randomly. Stamp the letters in medium blue and color them in.

Stamp the branch in gold ink. Randomly stamp branches on the lavender paper. Stamp the letters in gold on dark blue paper. Cut them into tiles.

Ink the coffee design roller in brown ink. Roll it over the paper. Ink the solid letters in darker brown and stamp out the word.

Create background paper by randomly stamping green and blue dots. Put the letter template over the background paper. Outline the letters with a marker. Cut out the letters. Adhere them to the dotted Swiss paper.

Stamp large As, Bs and Cs on paper and stamp off the same letters to create masks. Mask the letters. Stamp small As, Bs and Cs randomly. Remove the masks. Color in the big letters and re-outline them in black.

Roller Stamps

Beyond the flat stamps you know and love is a round, round world of roller stamps. These wheels of images snap onto a handle so you can run them over your paper.

Some roller stamps have inking cartridges that snap onto the handle. Others are a bit more tricky, since you have to ink the entire outside band or you'll wind up with a blank spot.

Concerned that you won't roll a straight line? Adapt my letter guide on page 47 to fit your roller and use it to guide your efforts.

Use roller stamps to:
• Create backgrounds.
• Make a border.
• Stamp on ribbon.
• Repeat an image with the same spacing across your paper.

SUPPLIES USED

Stamps:
Lasso Stamp by
Judi-Kins, © Carmen's
Veranda

Plant: Tiny Back-
grounds by Hero Arts

M.E. border

Miracle: Running Rhino
& Co. from Uptown
Rubber Stamps

Whisper Blue, Radiant
Pearl by Angelwing
Enterprises

Floral Lace Frame from
Uptown Rubber
Stamps

Holly Pond Hill,
© Susan Wheeler
Licensed by InterArt
Licensing

Pine Frame by All
Night Media

"Hugs and Kisses",
Kathy Davis Collection
from Inkadinkado

Inks:
Dauber Duos by
Tsukeniko

Stampin' Up

Pens, Pencils, Markers:
Marvy LePlume II
Berol
Micron by Sakura
Pentel Milky Gel Roller

Not Only a Frame, But a Line and a Corner and an "L"

Okay, you could use these stamps as photo frames or for journaling boxes. But why stop there? You've seen how many ways I used the leaf frame from the Menorah stamp. Why not isolate those pine cones? Frame a capital letter with the small lace border. Use the floral bouquet on the large lace as a photo corner. Stamp rows of hearts and draw the Xs and Os by hand. Cut off the bows from the rope frame and add them to a pair of stamped tennis shoes. What's stopping you?

TECHNIQUE: *Using Frame Stamps*

◀ Draw a light green pencil line to indicate the size and shape of your desired frame. Ink the greenery and stamp over the line until you have filled in a frame.

Use markers to ink in the frame and the leaves on this stamp. Stamp the image. Now dip a cotton swab into the Radiant Pearl and lightly rub it on the open spaces. ▶

◀ Ink the entire frame except where the letter K touches the border. Stamp the image. Color in the frame as desired. Use a marker to complete the lines around the frame.

Radiance for Paper in a Jar
This product is so beautiful that as soon as I saw them, I grabbed a handful of jars. A little bit of the solution goes a long way.

Clearly Radiant
One neat idea to highlight the translucent nature of Radiant Pearls is to stamp an image with pigment ink on an overhead projector transparency. Then emboss your image. The heat won't hurt the overhead cell since they are made to withstand high temperatures. Color your image in with Radiant Pearls. The final piece has the look of stained glass. Try it with a flower stamp, an angel stamp, or any stamp of a glass item such as a jar or vase.

Why Buying Stamps in a Set is a Great Idea

More and more rubber stamp companies offer their products in sets. The prices are reasonable, and less than what you would pay for the individual stamps. More importantly, stamps in a set give you more images to try. Often when you start stamping, you don't have enough different stamps to be creative. Or the stamps you have don't work together. The sets are designed so the stamps compliment each other. You don't have to match the style or size. I've heard people say, "I only want that one stamp, so I won't buy the set." However, what happens more often is you buy the set and the find an indispensible stamp you'd never have purchased.

TOOLBOX

SUPPLIES USED

Stamps:

1st border: © The Boyds Collection LTD Licensed by InterArt Licensing from Uptown Rubber Stamps™

Ribbon: © 1994 V.I.P.

2nd border: Lined paper, © 1998 Designs by Trena Hegdahl for Westwater Enterprises

Lace, cc Rubber Stamps

Play and Learn Stamp Letter Set by CraftsMate

3rd border: Key by OM Studio Seaside

Hearts by Rubber Stampede

Gold Jewel embossing powder by E.T.'s Rubber Stamps

4th border: Tiny Backgrounds by Hero Arts

5th border: Small Star of David, Fun Stamps by Stampendous

Dreidel punch by McGill

6th border: Gingerbread Man by All Night Media

Tiny Backgrounds by Hero Arts

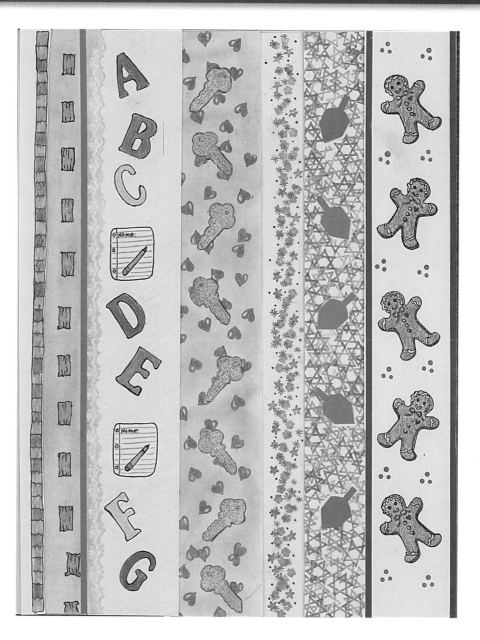

Goofs? I've Made More than My Share

Each one of these borders has a goof. On the far left ribbon the ink smeared as I colored it. You can see the crooked laced ribbon at the bottom of the next border. My letters didn't print perfectly on the alphabet strip. Until I outlined the keys in brown, they looked like gold globs. I cut right through the middle of the flowers, then fitted the pieces together and put tape on the back. My point? You don't have to be a perfect stamper to add great images and zest to your scrapbooking pages.

TECHNIQUE: *Creating Borders with Stamps*

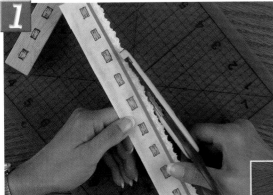

◀ Stamp the ribbon stamp in a line on your paper. Add the lace border, stamped in white. Emboss the lace. Go over the entire border with chalk. Add a Mrs. Grossman's Design Line sticker.

Stamp the letters A, B and C. Color ▶ them in. Ink the paper and pencil image with a marker so that the inside lines are blue and the outside lines are black. Stamp it. Touch up any lines as needed. Color in the paper and pencil stamp and the background.

Maximize Your Scrapping Time

Maybe you don't have time to attend a crop or a scrapping workshop, but you can get a lot of scrapping down by working on several pages at once. Carry around a stamped border or image and your colored pencils in a plastic bag. Color while you wait in the doctor's office, or in the student pick-up line at school or during practices.

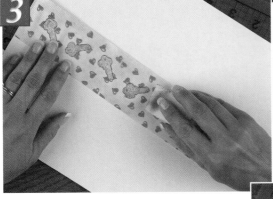

◀ Stamp the keys in gold ink and emboss them. Mask each key. Stamp the hearts randomly. Remove the masks. Outline the keys in brown. Cover the entire area with pink chalk.

Randomly stamp the Star of David ▶ stamp in blue and then in purple. Punch blue and purple dreidels. Affix the dreidels over the Star of David background.

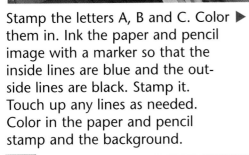

◀ Stamp gingerbread men. Add the red dots stamp. Color in the gingerbread men. Add Mrs. Grossman's Design Lines.

Index

Glossary of Terms

Archival—that which will not self-destruct or destroy other items over time.

Backstamping—the unintended image left behind by excess die material.

Bleed—extending an image off the edges of the page.

Chalk—a colored calcium carbonate substance used to mark on paper.

Corner template—a pattern for creating a folded paper sleeve designed to hold a photo or a square of paper on paper.

Chuff— to blow moist air onto a die to reactivate the ink.

Craft knife—a tool with a replaceable blade that is used for cutting.

Dauber Duo—a brand name for a double-sided round ink pad.

Deckle scissors—decorative scissors with an irregular blade.

Design Line (by Mrs. Grossman)—a brand name sticker tape that comes in colors.

Die—an engraved or cut out piece used to impress an image (the face of a stamp).

Die cut—a paper image punched out by a metal die.

Dye ink—a fast drying coloring substance.

Embellishment—a page element added for decorative purposes.

Embossing gun—a heat emitting instrument for raising embossing powder.

Embossing powder—a powder that rises when heated.

Foam stamp—a device of spongy material created to impress an image.

Handle—the portion of the stamp created to help you manipulate the die.

HERMAfix—a brand name adhesive that rolls on in small dots, is repositionable, and is easily removed.

Index—the printed image on the handle of your stamp.

Interactive stamps—stamps designed to work together to create images.

Journaling—writing or telling your story.

Journaling boxes—areas where journaling will go.

Layout—the design of elements on a scrapbook page.

Liquid applique—paint that rises in height after application.

Marrying color—the technique of borrowing color from one area and adding it to another to create visual harmony.

Masking—covering one image to protect it while adding another image to a page.

Matting—backing a photo or page element with a second piece of paper.

Off stamping—impressing an image multiple times without re-inking.

Photo split—(photo stickers) double-sided tape squares for securing page elements.

Pigment ink—slow drying coloring substance.

Post-it Note—a brand name for repositionable paper product by 3M.

Punch—a hand held tool using a metal die to cut shapes.

Radiant Pearl—a brand name for an opalescent ink.

Rainbow ink page—a felt inking system with a variety of colors on one surface.

Roller stamps— a handle and die system that prints an image by rolling it onto a surface.

Rubber stamps—stamps with rubber dies.

Score—to create an indented line for folding.

Silhouette cropping—cutting away the background from a photo.

Stamping—using a device to impress an image.

Stamping markers—ink filled markers with die cut tips to be used as stamps.

Stamping off—see *off stamping*

Stampin' Up—a company that manufacturers and distributes stamps and stamping products.

Stencil—a lightweight cut pattern used as a guide. See also *Template*

Stippling—the process of laying down ink or color with a quick up and down tapping motion.

Template—a cut pattern to be used as a guide. (Although stencil and template are often used interchangeably, a template is typically a heavier weight than a stencil.)

Thought bubble—a cartoon used to illustrate a mental image or phrase.

Tick—a small, light mark.

Tile lettering—individual letters in square shapes.

Vellum—a high quality translucent paper.

Waste paper or **trash paper**—paper unsuitable for use in a scrapbook.

Water color pencils—pencils with water soluble lead.

Waterbase markers—coloring tools that are water soluble.

Waterproof markers—coloring tools that are water resistant.

A Mini Bonus Gallery...

Happy Camper

Paint by Delta; Rustic Letter template by Frances Meyer; tree stencil by Pebbles; pencils by Berol.

Ladybug—Fly Away Home

Paint by Delta; Oak Leaf foam stamp by Chucky Stamps, Back Street Inc.; font Contemporary Capitals and script by CK; pen by Avery

I'm No Snow Angel!

Celestial Angel stamp © Cheryl Darrow and Sara Crittendon of Uptown Rubber Stamps; snow stamp by Stamp Oasis; ink by Dauber Duos by Tsukineko; Zany Zoo Sky paper Fayette Skinner for Provo Craft; script font by CK; markers by Fibracolor

Other Titles for Scrapbookers and Storytellers...

ISBN: 1-930500-01-7
80 pages (2001); $14.99

Quick & Easy Pages

Save more memories in less time

If you've ever wished you had more time to scrapbook, or didn't think you had the time to start, this is the one book you must buy. Joanna Slan shares easy ways to present photographs, pull together your pages and title any page. You'll learn over a hundred speedy scrapbooking techniques along with dozens of money-saving tips. Great how-to photos guide you through every step.

Coming Spring 2001:

ISBN: 1-930500-03-3
80 pages (2001); $14.99

One Minute Journaling shows how to capture your stores as they're happening using one-minute journaling methods. Then, you'll see how to get your stories onto your pages in under a minute!

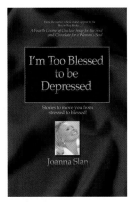

ISBN: 0-9630222-8-8
128 pages (1999); $19.99

Scrapbook Storytelling

Save family stories and memories with photos, journaling and your own creativity

See how to document stories—from a quick sentence to page after scrapbook page. The book is full of ways to recover stories from the past, discover the stories in the present and create stories that light the path to the future.

With easily understood steps for documenting stories, readers then choose to combine narrative with photos, journals, memorabilia and more.

ISBN: 0-9630222-7-X
128 pages (1998); $19.99

Creating Family Newsletters

123 ideas for sharing memorable moments with family and friends

Creating Family Newsletters contains ideas and inspiration that makes a newsletter "doable" by anyone, regardless of age or writing and design ability. Through over 123 color examples, you'll see which type of newsletter is for you—text-only, poems, photo scrapbooks, cards, letters, genealogy, e-mail or Web sites.

ISBN: 1-930500-04-1
208 pages (2001); $14.99

I'm Too Blessed to be Depressed is filled with inspirational stories and guided journaling that provide the perfect prescription for the blues.

? STORY STARTERS

If you've enjoyed the Story Starters throughout this book, be sure to sign up at www.scrapbookstorytelling.com for my free monthly broadcast of more ideas. Click the Free Newsletter button on the home page.

File Edit View Go Bookmarks Communicator Help

Netscape: Scrapbook Storytelling

Back Forward Reload Home Search Netscape Images Print Security Shop Stop

Location: http://www.scrapbookstorytelling.com/

Tips
Page Ideas
New Products
Events
Templates
Suppliers
Contact Us

Scrapbook Storytelling

Your link to saving everyday stories with Joanna Campbell Slan

Free Newsletter

Scrapping Snippets

What's New?

Its All Greek to Me ... Here's the Greeking that Joanna Slan mentioned in this month's issue of Creating Keepsakes. Copy and paste it into a word processing file. Consider naming the file "Greeking" so you can easily find it when you need it to hold a journaling space for your scrapbook pages.

Question of the Month ... How do you handle awkward stories in your scrapbook?

There are often stories we want to save for future generations but may not want them on our coffee table. Joanna shares some ideas.

Attention Scrapbook Store Owners ... If you are interested in carrying Joanna's books in your store, please e-mail us at savetales@aol.com so we can provide you with wholesale information and other special goodies to help you and your customers save stories.

Are you ready for more ideas on storytelling... Joanna is working fast and furiously this summer on two new books for scrapbookers, Storytelling with Rubber Stamps and Quick & Easy Pages. Reserve your copies today.

Sign up to receive monthly Story Starters from Joanna Slan and news as the site is updated.

This is NOT the end. It's just the beginning!

Let's keep in touch—Visit my Web site at http://www.scrapbookstorytelling.com

There, you'll find the templates mentioned in this book, new page ideas, tips and more! Plus, you'll be the first to know about my new products, free templates, and free monthly Story Starters by e-mail.

The story continues... and you can be a part of it.